Contemporary Readings in Psychology
A New York Times Reader

Contemporary Readings in Psychology
A New York Times Reader

Erik J. Coats
Vassar College

Prentice Hall
Upper Saddle River, New Jersey 07458

Library of Congress Cataloging-in-Publication Data

Contemporary readings in psychology: a New York times reader / [edited by] Erik J. Coats. — 1st ed.
p. cm.
ISBN 0-13-977513-7
1. Psychology. I. Coats, Erik J., 1968– . II. New York times.
BF121.C622 2000
150—dc21
99-40328
CIP

Editorial Director: Charlyce Jones-Owen
Editor-in-Chief: Nancy Roberts
Executive Editor: Bill Webber
Acquisitions Editor: Jennifer Cohen
AVP and Director of Production and Manufacturing: Barbara Kittle
Managing Editor: Mary Rottino
Editorial/Production Supervisor: Lisa M. Guidone
Manufacturing Manager: Nick Sklitsis
Prepress and Manufacturing Buyer: Tricia Kenny
Marketing Director: Gina Sluss
Marketing Manager: Sharon Cosgrove
Cover Designer: Bruce Kenselaar
Copyeditor: Kathy Pruno
Proofreader: Bennie Sauls

This book was set in 10/12 Meridien by Pub-Set, Inc.
and was printed by Courier-Westford.
The cover was printed by Phoenix Color Corp.

Printed in the United States of America

10 9 8 7 6 5 4 3 2 1

0-13-977513-7

Prentice-Hall International (UK) Limited, *London*
Prentice-Hall of Australia Pty. Limited, *Sydney*
Prentice-Hall Canada Inc., *Toronto*
Prentice-Hall Hispanoamericana, S.A., *Mexico*
Prentice-Hall of India Private Limited, *New Delhi*
Prentice-Hall of Japan, Inc., *Tokyo*
Pearson Education Asia Pte. Ltd., *Singapore*
Editora Prentice-Hall do Brasil, Ltda., *Rio de Janeiro*

*Contents**

---

*See the Preface for a description of the organization of the Contents.

Section V
Psychopathology and Its Treatment
(See also Readings 5, 8, 11, and 19) *101*

Preface

Why This Book Was Written

To introduce students to cutting edge data and theory. Primary textbooks do, of course, include the newest ideas and data. But textbook authors do not usually include the most cutting edge ideas and data. And for good reason—as a scientific discipline, psychologists are cautious about accepting the ideas put forth in one study until that study can be successfully repeated (or replicated). Although it may be tempting for a textbook author to include the newest and most sensational breaking news about psychology in their books, they resist and focus, instead, on ideas that have stood the test of time. It would be reckless to introduce readers to the newest ideas in psychology before they were sufficiently grounded in established principles or replicated by other researchers in the field.

But wouldn't it be interesting to see what is going on at the forefront of psychology? Wouldn't it be interesting to see what new theories are competing to replace older ones? This book is intended for people who agree that it would—people interested in how psychology is evolving, changing, and being applied to new problems and issues.

To help students become more savvy consumers of psychology in the popular press. Introductory psychology is one of the most, if not the most, popular courses in colleges and universities today. Yet few of the thousands of people who take a first course in psychology will ever take a second. Fewer still will decide to major in psychology, and only a small fraction will pursue a psychology-related career. The millions of students who take only one course in psychology will, however, continue to be exposed to new theory and data in the field. They will keep in touch with psychology not by reading articles in scientific journals, but by reading newspapers, listening to news on the radio, and watching news programs on television. This book is intended for these people—people who will continue to be interested in psychology throughout their adult lives but will not pursue it as a career.

Every medium has its own style. Undergraduates who major in psychology learn something of the style of journal articles in the psychological sciences. An intimate knowledge of this medium is essential to people who pursue psychology as a career. But not to the rest of the world. The intelligent nonpsychologist needs to know the style of the popular press, which is quite different. Whereas journal articles are cautious in interpreting new findings, the popular press tends to exaggerate new findings, treating tentative ideas as if they were more universally accepted than they are. Consequently, reading about psychology in the popular press requires greater caution and skepticism than reading a journal article or textbook.

The articles in this book all appeared first in *The New York Times*. Reading *The Times* is an excellent way for nonpsychologists to keep up with current trends in the field. *The Times* is among the most reliable of newspapers when it comes to writing about the psychological sciences. Still, the knowledgeable reader should read *The Times* with a questioning mind. Are the data reported sufficient to support the theory being presented? What assumptions are being made by the researcher or reporter and are they supported? Can this new theory explain previously observed facts?

How This Book Is Organized

There are five main sections in this book that contain five readings each. *Section I* includes articles about the neurobiological basis of human behavior; *Section II* articles that focus on consciousness and cognitive psychology; *Section III* articles on issues of human development; *Section IV* articles on personality and social psychology; and *Section V* articles on psychopathology and its treatment. The division of articles into these five sections is somewhat arbitrary, and articles often bridge multiples areas of psychology. When an article deals with topics in multiple areas, it was placed in the section that seemed most appropriate and a notation was added to let you know to what other section it is relevant. For example, reading 2 is about the neurological basis of memory. It is included in Section I because of its focus on neurobiology, but the notation "(II)" appears after the title to indicate it is also relevant to Section II: Consciousness and Cognition. To further help you identify cross-disciplinary articles, the Contents indicates for each section what other readings are relevant. For example, the heading for Section I tells you that readings 7 and 23 are also relevant to the neurobiology of human behavior.

Each of the 25 readings in this book are preceded by a short introduction and followed by five critical thinking questions. The introduction provides background about the issues that will be addressed in the reading. More complete background is likely in your textbook, although texts do differ in their content and yours may not discuss all of the topics brought up in this book. The questions that follow each reading are intended to make sure that you understand the central issues of the article and to challenge you to think critically about the reading. I strongly encourage you to answer each question. You will not be helped as much by these questions if you merely give a short mental answer to yourself. You will be helped far more if you write out a detailed answer or, better still, discuss your answers with a classmate.

Section I
Neurobiology of Human Behavior

Reading 1

Fear and Anger Heard Deep Inside the Brain

Introduction

Advances in our understanding of the biological basis of behavior often come from case studies of people who have brain abnormalities. Because it is not ethical to damage a healthy brain intentionally in order to see the resulting effect on behavior, scientists must wait for natural causes (for example, a tumor or head injury) to result in brain damage. Then by carefully observing changes in behavior following damage to a specific brain area, we gain insight into the normal function of that area.

This first reading reports a case study of a woman whose brain was damaged intentionally but for her own benefit. Some cases of severe epilepsy do not respond to drug therapy, and in the most severe cases the radical approach of removing part of the brain is the preferred course of treatment. In such surgeries, doctors first identify what brain area seems to be causing the seizures, and then they remove it. Sometimes this psychosurgery includes cutting the corpus callosum connecting the two hemispheres of the brain. In the case described here, however, the patient's seizures seemed to originate in the amygdala. Surgeons therefore removed it.

You may recall that the amygdala is part of the limbic system in the midbrain. The amygdala has for some time been known to be involved in aggression. For example, the mass murderer Charles Whitman (who shot 16 people from atop the clock tower at the University of Texas at Austin) had a brain tumor that affected this region of his brain. But observations of people who have had their amygdala removed suggests that its influence is more broad than just aggression. It now appears that this small organ is involved in multiple aspects of the emotions fear and anger.

SANDRA BLAKESLEE*
JANUARY 21, 1997

Scientists have new evidence that the human brain contains a special structure for detecting fear and anger, two emotions that underlie much of human behavior: a woman with damage to the structure, called the amygdala, cannot hear intonations of fear or anger in other people's voices.

Previous research showed that patients with amygdala damage had difficulty recognizing facial expressions of fear and anger, said Dr. Andrew Young, a professor at the Medical Research Council Applied Psychology Unit in Cambridge, England. This is the first time it has been shown in humans that the amygdala also processes the emotional content of auditory information, he said. The amygdala is involved in the overall appraisal of danger and the emotion of fear, regardless of the sensory input, said Dr. Young, the lead author of a study on the woman. The report appears in the current issue of the journal *Nature.*

"It is an interesting finding that adds to ongoing knowledge about how the amygdala is related to emotions," said Dr. Antonio Damasio, a neuroscientist at the University of Iowa.

Dr. Joseph LeDoux, an expert on emotions at New York University, said: "It's a very important finding. We know a lot about the amygdala in animals and its role in the detection and response to danger." This human study, he said, is in strong agreement with the animal research.

The amygdala is a peanut-size nucleus found deep in the midbrain. Because the human brain has two separate hemispheres, each person has two amygdalas, one on each side.

The patient, a woman in her early 50's, began having epileptic attacks at the age of 28. When the seizures could not be controlled with medicine, she underwent several operations that removed much of the tissue from both her amygdalas.

She lives a normal life, Dr. Young said, with the help of a protective husband. She understands the meaning of emotion and can describe circumstances in which other people will experience feelings like happiness, sadness and anger. She can recall, from memory, what it is like to feel afraid. Her only complaint is that she will sometimes feel fear when no one else does or she will not feel it when she probably should, he said.

---

*Reprinted with permission from *The New York Times.*

The new study tested her ability to interpret the emotional content of sounds, including human voices.

In one experiment, the woman heard single words, like "carpet," which, in their meaning, carried no emotional content. But the words were spoken in tones of happiness, sadness, anger, fear or disgust. The patient had the most trouble with fear and anger, Dr. Young said. She was slightly better at identifying the other emotions.

In a second experiment, the woman heard sounds associated with emotions, like laughter for happiness and growling for anger. Again, she had the most trouble recognizing anger and fear but performed normally for the other emotions.

The amygdala plays an important role in social cognition, Dr. Young said, and is especially evolved for interpreting fear and anger. This makes evolutionary sense, he said, in that people need a way to recognize fear and anger in other people, to know that there is immediate danger in the environment.

Displays of fear and anger by other people are signals for the presence of an immediate threat in the environment, and anger carries a clear intention to frighten the recipient, he said. People do not have to learn anew each time why things are life-threatening.

The role of the amygdala is to set off fear and anger instantly, without conscious thought, so that a person can freeze or run away from danger, Dr. Young said. But the emotion of fear does not reside exclusively in the amygdala because it can be elicited from memory and other brain states.

QUESTIONS

1. Why has it taken so long for neuroscientists to make this seemingly straightforward discovery?
2. How would a psychologist categorize the methodology of the study reported in this reading? What problems can occur with this methodology?
3. How do we know that the amygdala is less involved in emotions other than fear and anger? Does the evidence seem compelling to you?
4. From an evolutionary perspective, what selective pressures might have shaped the formation of the amygdala?
5. Can you posit an explanation for why the woman discussed in this article does occasionally experience fear?

Reading 2

Doctors Record Signals of Brain Cells Linked to Memory

Introduction

This second reading, like the first, highlights an advance in basic research made while coping with the applied problem of reducing epileptic seizures. Recall that in the first reading doctors gained insights into the normal function of the amygdala by observing the behavior of a woman whose amygdala was removed during surgery. Nicholas Wade's article highlights a newer and more precise method of studying brain function, one that does not require removing any part of the brain. This new method allows psychologists to study areas of the brain without having to wait for a natural occurrence to result in its removal or damage.

Recall that during the first stage of surgery to alleviate seizures, neurosurgeons must identify the region of the brain most responsible for the seizures. This requires a long process of electrically stimulating the various regions of the brain until they hit on the area that set off a seizure (the patients must be awake during this probing!). During this discovery process, one research team made a provocative finding about cells in the hippocampus.

Surgeries performed decades ago demonstrated conclusively that the hippocampus—the horse-shaped structure found in the brain's limbic system—is crucial in forming new long-term memories, but exactly how it stores memories is still something of a mystery. But existing technology—including the latest technologies for scanning the brain (the PET and MRI)—cannot answer precise questions of how cells communicate to encode (i.e., store) information. Such questions might be answered, however, using the kind of open-brain experiments described in this reading.

Nicholas Wade*
May 24, 1997

A team of neurosurgeons say that in preparing epilepsy patients for operation, they have recorded signals from single human brain cells that make the associations leading to long-term memories, the first time that feat has been achieved.

In some cases the cells seemed to know better than their owner, since they responded positively to a photograph of a face that the researchers had already shown but that the patient denied having seen before.

The tests were performed by Drs. Itzhak Fried, Katherine A. MacDonald and Charles L. Wilson of the University of California at Los Angeles in the course of pinpointing the source regions of epilepsy in a series of patients. The results were published yesterday in the journal *Neuron.*

The nerve cells were situated in a structure of the brain called the hippocampus. Patients whose hippocampus has been removed retain memories from before the operation but cannot form new ones, suggesting that the hippocampus is required for forming long-term memories but is not a site of permanent storage.

Ethical opportunities to record from the human hippocampus are very rare, and a previous effort did not capture the associations that, given past work with rodents and monkeys, Dr. Fried and his colleagues thought they would see.

New methods of scanning the brain have helped locate many of its functions, but these scanning methods measure blood flow to active regions and do not reveal just how brain cells encode information. That requires recording directly from a nerve cell by sticking an electrode into it, as the Fried team did.

An emerging feature of knowledge about the brain is that incoming information is separated into many different strands. For instance, faces, letters and colors are processed in different areas of the cortex, the thin sheet of nerve cells that makes up the outer surface of the brain. Even for faces, special attributes like identity, expression and sex are represented in different parts of the cortex. An outstanding problem for brain scientists is to explain how these separately processed attributes are brought together.

In terms of long-term memory, the hippocampus, a structure with intimate connections to many regions of the cortex, has long seemed cast for a leading role in bringing together separate attributes.

Studies with rats and mice have uncovered the remarkable phenomenon of what are called "place cells" in the hippocampus. When the mouse enters a strange environment, many hippocampal cells are recruited to record the new scene. Researchers recording signals from the cells can tell where the mouse is in its cage by looking to see which cell is firing. Discovery of the place cells set up a debate among neuroscientists. Some say that forming spatial memories is the main role of the hippocampus. Others contend that this may be

---

true in rats and mice, for which space is important, but that in humans the hippocampus has a much broader role.

The new data reported by Dr. Fried and his colleagues support the second view. Figuring that humans are very oriented toward recognizing individual faces and their expressions, and that faces would be as important to humans as spaces are to rats, Dr. Fried showed a set of faces expressing different emotions to his wired-up patients. He recorded responses from the hippocampus cells both when the faces were being identified for the first time, and when they were recognized or otherwise on a second showing.

A fair number of the cells responded singly to conjunctions of various attributes. For example, one cell responded to the expression of anger in two different faces. Others responded strongly to faces that were both new and wearing angry expressions.

"This is the first time in the human that we have seen this type of conjunctive coding," Dr. Fried said.

Of particular note were cells that responded positively to a previously seen face, even though the patients said they did not remember having seen the face before. In possible explanation of that strange result, Dr. Fried said that "we are essentially probing into very large networks of cells" and that the conscious decision of whether a face has been seen before "is probably a matter of voting" among the cells. In other words, the cell his electrode had happened to hit said aye on the question of recognition but may have been outvoted by other cells in the network.

Several experts said the new result was important because it established that the hippocampus has a role in humans similar to that found in rodents and monkeys, thus confirming that these animals are good guides for studying the human brain.

"It's a very nice confirmation of the similarity across species," said Dr. Howard B. Eichenbaum of Boston University.

QUESTIONS

1. What evidence suggests that the hippocampus is involved in forming new memories but not in storing memories?
2. To what is Fried referring when he says their study is the first to show evidence of "conjunctive coding"?
3. How can a person incorrectly report not recalling a target face even though an individual neuron in the hippocampus correctly recalls seeing the target face?
4. Why are the newest brain scan technologies unable to answer the questions that Fried and his team pose in this reading?
5. Outline one similarity and one difference in the function of the hippocampus in humans and mice. What are the implications of this for animal research aimed at understanding human behavior?

Reading 3

Hardest Habit to Break: Memories of the High

Introduction

The practice of trying to understand human behavior by focusing on its precise neurobiological concomitants—an approach referred to as biological reductionism—has had a number of impressive successes in recent years. By identifying the biological basis of a behavior, it is often possible to alter the behavior using a biological intervention. The most common biological intervention is drug therapy, and in recent years new drugs have been developed to combat behavior problems that have never responded well to behavior-oriented psychotherapies. Today drug therapies are among the most effective ways to help people cope with depression, anxiety, mood swings, and a host of other ailments. The following reading reports work being done around the country aimed at producing a new class of drugs that might someday be effective in treating yet another behavior problem. Ironically, this new drug is being developed to treat psychological craving for drugs.

The idea of using one drug to help reduce our body's craving for another drug is not new; methadone is routinely given to heroin addicts. But the research reported in this reading is more complex. The aim of these scientists is not to replace one craving for another, but to design a drug that would eliminate cravings for drugs entirely. This lofty goal is still years away, but advances in our basic understanding of neurobiology are bringing it closer all the time.

DENISE GRADY*
OCTOBER 27, 1998

As anyone who has tried to quit smoking knows, it is much easier to get off an addictive drug than to stay off it. That applies to virtually all addicts and all types of addictions, whether to alcohol, cocaine, heroin, nicotine or amphetamines. Long after the drug is cleared from the body, it retains a powerful hold on the mind, and despite weeks, months or sometimes even years of abstinence, cravings can linger or suddenly make a shattering comeback. The usual, devastating, consequence is relapse.

"Prolonged drug use changes the brain in fundamental and lasting ways," said Dr. Alan Leshner, director of the National Institute on Drug Abuse. Those long-term effects are not well understood, Dr. Leshner said, and learning more about them may lead to new treatments that offer lasting help to addicts.

Help is certainly needed: The institute estimates that 4 million Americans are drug addicts, including 2 million to 3 million hooked on cocaine and 800,000 on heroin. Millions more, though not addicted, use illegal drugs, and 14 million are alcoholics.

Compared with people who have other mental or physical disorders, addicts have few treatments to choose from. No drug treatment is available for cocaine addiction. Methadone helps some heroin addicts, but by no means all, and two other drugs are useful in only a minority of alcoholics.

In recent years, much addiction research has focused on the reinforcing, or pleasure-producing properties of drugs, which have been traced to their ability to flood certain parts of the brain with *dopamine,* a substance that nerve cells use to communicate with each other. But even though the rise and fall of dopamine can alter brain cells in ways that contribute to craving, researchers do not think those alterations explain all the long-term mental effects of drug abuse. And there has been no payoff in terms of treatment, in part because the dopamine system is so fundamental to so many types of pleasure that tampering with it to treat addiction may take all the joy out of life.

As a result, the emphasis in addiction research has begun to shift, to move beyond the dopamine pleasure centers to other systems in the brain. "We've learned a lot about reinforcement," said Dr. Eric J. Nestler, an addiction researcher at Yale University. "But there are other aspects to an addict's life also, having to do with memory and conditioning. Maybe the time is ripe to examine those."

Some changes in the brains of addicts resemble changes that take place in healthy people when certain types of memories are formed.

---

*Reprinted with permission from *The New York Times.*

In some cases, Dr. Nestler's research has shown, those changes even include alterations in the functioning of genes.

Dr. Alcino Silva, who studies memory at the University of California at Los Angeles, said, "Addiction may hijack natural systems used for learning and memory."

Addiction researchers have begun to pay particular attention to "emotional memories," which, as the name suggests, are the mental records of events that aroused intense emotions, either wonderful or terrible.

"Emotional memories are very powerful, and they're the ones that remain with you the longest," said Dr. Jonathan Pollock, a program officer at the institute. "You remember where you were when Kennedy was assassinated or the Challenger disaster happened. You remember very pleasurable events in your life, like your wedding or the first time you got an A in school."

The intensity of the moment helps to burn emotional memories into brain circuits. The memories are encoded into a part of the brain that operates outside conscious control, and they seem to take on a life of their own, sometimes intruding on the mind when they are not wanted. When emotional memories are reactivated, touched off perhaps by a smell, a taste, a snatch of music, the sight of an old friend or some other signal that a person may not even be consciously aware of, they can evoke the same powerful emotions that helped form them.

Many addiction researchers believe memories of being high on drugs fall into this category of emotional memories, and contribute to craving, compulsion and relapse.

Although a relapse can occur for no apparent reason, many addicts say that cravings are brought on by cues or reminders of past drug use, like seeing a needle or crack pipe or visiting a place where they used to get high.

Stress can also rekindle cravings. So, in many people, can just one hit of an addicting drug, even after a long abstinence. The obsessive thoughts that follow, Dr. Leshner said, are "the very definition of an emotional memory."

Last month, Dr. Pollock invited 15 researchers to the National Institutes of Health in Bethesda, Md., to discuss the possible role of emotional memory in addiction. He said it was the first time that experts on addiction and experts on memory had been brought together, and at the start of the meeting Dr. Leshner gave the scientists a firm agenda: "What I'm worried about is compulsion. I only care about compulsion."

Much of the interest in emotional memory stems from studies by Dr. Joseph LeDoux, a researcher at New York University. Working with rats that have been trained by means of electrical shocks to fear a certain sound—a response that qualifies as an emotional memory—he has found that emotional memories are formed in the amygdala, an almond-shaped structure deep within the brain.

The job of the amygdala, Dr. LeDoux said, is to react instantly when it detects a danger signal—the sound, in the case of the rats—sending out messages that prepare the body for fight or flight and that create a state of fear. The human amygdala works in much the same way. It reacts in a few thousandths of a second, independent of the cortex of the brain, which means that people may respond to cues that they are not consciously aware of.

Although Dr. LeDoux has worked mainly on fear, that is not all the amygdala mediates. It includes 13 areas, called nuclei, only two of which are known to be involved in fear. The other areas may process other types of emotional memory.

"The amygdala is showing up in a lot of addiction studies," Dr. LeDoux said.

When addicts who say they are in the throes of a craving are given brain scans, the images suggest that the amygdala is involved, according to studies by Dr. Hans Breiter of the Massachusetts General Hospital and Dr. Annarose Childress of the University of Pennsylvania in Philadelphia.

Other researchers, working with animals, have also found that the amygdala is important in responding to cues associated with rewards like cocaine and food. Dr. Barry Everitt, a psychology professor at the University of Cambridge in England, said that an "amazing property" of stimulant drugs like cocaine and amphetamines was their capacity to stimulate exceptionally powerful responses to cues that have been associated with them. "They amplify the control of behavior by environmental events," Dr. Everitt said.

Dr. Michaela Gallagher of Johns Hopkins University in Baltimore suggested that drug abuse might also affect the cortex of the brain, inhibiting a region that would normally help keep the amygdala in check. That, she said, may make the amygdala extra responsive to all sorts of environmental cues, including those associated with drugs.

Other factors may also give cues more power to evoke emotional memories, according to research by Dr. Jane Stewart of Concordia University in Montreal. One is stress, which increases levels in the brain of a hormone called C.R.F., or corticotropin releasing factor, which may act on the amygdala.

"Dr. Stewart and her colleagues are showing that C.R.F., released during stress, causes anxiety," Dr. Leshner said. "Maybe C.R.F. released during abstinence exaggerates anxiety in addicts. We're going to look at things that block C.R.F. to see if that will help. We haven't tried it in humans yet, but it has been done in animals. It looks good to me, and we're in negotiations with a pharmaceutical company about it, and we'll run clinical trials."

Ultimately, Dr. Leshner said, he expects that treatment of addiction would combine behavioral therapy and drugs that combat craving and compulsion. Addicts may not be able to control their cravings, but therapy may teach them to control the way they respond to them.

Questions

1. What evidence suggested to Leshner that drug use affects the brain in "fundamental and lasting ways"?
2. If dopamine is responsible for drug cravings, why don't treatments focus on controlling levels of this neurotransmitter?
3. What evidence or observation led researchers to treat memories of being high as emotional memories?
4. Why, according to the theory posited in this reading, is our memory for emotional events better than it is for nonemotional events? Can you suggest an alternative explanation for this?
5. What types of emotional events are known to be processed by the amygdala (review reading 1)? Is this consistent with drug cravings being associated with activation of this region? Is this consistent with LeDoux's supposition that "memories of the high" are formed in this area?

Reading 4

When an Adult Adds a Language, It's One Brain, Two Systems

Introduction

Many people have referred to the 1990s in psychology as the decade of the brain. The past few years have seen a plethora of new discoveries in brain function and operation. One of the chief reasons for this recent boom is new advances in brain-scanning technology. Although these technologies are limited in the kinds of questions they can answer (see reading 2) by allowing researchers to see what areas of the brain are consuming oxygen at any given moment, they provide us with a window onto brain activity. One such technology is magnetic resonance imaging (MRI). This device provides a noninvasive method of identifying the function of different brain areas in the cortex. The advantages of the MRI over brain surgery (as reported in readings 2 and 3) are clear. It is far easier, faster, and cheaper to conduct MRI research (and to recruit participants for research!).

In this next reading, neurologists use the MRI to identify the areas of the brain active when bilinguals process language. Specifically, they are interested to know whether the same area of the brain processes both languages or whether different areas are devoted to the different languages. They discover that the answer to this question depends on when in life the second language was learned.

Sandra Blakeslee*
July 15, 1997

As thousands of teen-agers who have struggled to engrave high school French on recalcitrant neurons might have guessed, a new study has found that second languages are stored differently in the human brain depending on when they are learned.

Babies who learn two languages simultaneously, and apparently effortlessly, have a single brain region for generating complex speech, researchers say. But people who learn a second language in adolescence or adulthood possess two such brain regions, one for each language.

The findings, described in the current issue of the journal *Nature*, shed new light on some notoriously difficult questions about brain development: How does the brain organize language in infancy and how are multiple languages represented in the brain? Why do some brain regions appear immutable after childhood, while others appear flexible and malleable in adult life? Why are languages harder to learn later in life?

There have always been strong hints that the brain can use separate brain regions for first and second languages, said Dr. Michael Posner, a psychologist at the University of Oregon in Eugene. Bilingual epilepsy patients may, during seizures, lose the ability to speak one language and not another. A stroke victim can permanently lose the ability to speak French but retain English or another language. "But it's not been known how these separate language areas form in the brain," Dr. Posner said. "Are the languages fused? Do they prime one another? Is one translated by another?"

The new study shows for the first time that two languages can be mapped in common neural tissue, Dr. Posner said, adding, "It is very helpful for understanding bilingualism."

The research was carried out by Dr. Joy Hirsch, head of Memorial Sloan-Kettering Hospital's functional MRI Laboratory and her graduate student, Karl Kim. Functional magnetic resonance imaging, or MRI, is a relatively new, noninvasive brain imaging technique that can pinpoint exactly which parts of the brain are active during cognitive tasks such as talking, seeing, waving an arm or daydreaming. Brain surgeons at the hospital are now using the technique to identify critical brain regions so that they will not do more harm than good when removing a tumor or other abnormality.

Of these critical regions, language is perhaps at the top of the list, said Dr. Philip H. Gutin, the hospital's chief of neurosurgery. Some functions such as seeing and hearing are located in both brain hemispheres, he said. When a tumor forms, surgeons can cut out tissue and not do great harm because the other side of the brain will take over. "But language is a high-rent district,"

Dr. Gutin said. Some high-level aspects of language tend to be found only on one side of the brain. By removing a spot of tissue smaller than an eraser, a surgeon could excise a crucial region of language production and destroy a person's ability to speak or understand English.

Moreover, language areas are never found in exactly the same spot, Dr. Gutin said. These regions are formed in childhood as language is acquired and are in slightly different spots in different people. Given that a quarter of all brain tumors occur in regions of the brain where language skills might reside, accurate imaging is a must, he said.

To explore where languages lie in the brain, Dr. Hirsch recruited 12 healthy bilingual people from New York City. Ten different languages were represented in the group. Half had learned two languages in infancy. The other half began learning a second language around age 11 and had acquired fluency by 19 after living in the country where the language was spoken. With their heads inside the MRI machine, subjects thought silently about what they had done the day before using complex sentences, first in one language, then in the other. The machine detected increases in blood flow, indicating where in the brain this thinking took place.

Aspects of language ability are distributed all over the brain, Dr. Hirsch said. But there are some high-level, executive regions that are usually localized in a certain neighborhood on the left side of the brain, but are sometimes found in the same neighborhood on the right side, or on both sides. One is Wernicke's area, a region devoted to understanding the meaning of words and the subject matter of spoken language, or semantics. Another is Broca's area, a region dedicated to the execution of speech as well as some deep grammatical aspects of language. The regions are identified by observing brain function.

None of the 12 bilinguals had two separate Wernicke's areas, Dr. Hirsch said. In an English and Spanish speaker, for instance, Spanish semantics blended with English semantics in the same area. But there were dramatic differences in Broca's areas, Dr. Hirsch said. In people who had learned both languages in infancy, there was only one uniform Broca's region for both languages, a dot of tissue containing about 30,000 neurons. Among those who had learned a second language in adolescence, however, Broca's area seemed to be divided into two distinct areas. Only one area was activated for each language. These two areas lay close to each other but were always separate, Dr. Hirsch said, and the second language area was always about the same size as the first language area.

This implies that the brain uses different strategies for learning languages, depending on age, Dr. Hirsch said. A baby learns to talk using all faculties—hearing, vision, touch and movement—which may feed into hardwired circuits like Broca's area. Once cells in this region become tuned to one or more languages, they become fixed. If two languages are acquired at this time, they become intermingled.

But people who learn a second language in high school have to acquire new skills for generating the complex speech sounds of the new tongue, which may explain why a second language is harder to learn. Broca's area is already dedicated to the native tongue and so an ancillary Broca's region is created. But Wernicke's area, which handles the simpler semantic aspects of language, can overlap.

Questions

1. What previous evidence suggested that bilinguals might process the two languages in two different areas of the brain?
2. Why does Gutin call language a "high rent area"? What makes processing language different from processing visual images?
3. On what side of the brain are Wernicke's and Broca's areas usually found?
4. Do these results imply that it would be easier to learn to speak a second language in adolescence or to learn to understand a second language?
5. What do these results suggest about the difficulty of learning a third language in adolescence after two were learned in childhood?

Reading 5

First Gene for Social Behavior Identified in Whiskery Mice

Introduction

As mentioned in the introduction to reading 3, biological reductionism often provides valuable insights into human behavior. Because the insights gained from biological reductionism most often complement those gained from other approaches, this approach is most often used in combination with others. For example, examining the phenomenon of depression at the biological level revealed that depression is associated with low levels of the two neurotransmitters serotonin and epinephrine. This discovery led to new drugs to combat depression, such as Prozac. In this case biological reductionism resulted in a new treatment. But finding a correlation between depression and low levels of certain neurotransmitters does not necessarily mean that levels of neurotransmitters are the cause of depression. Depression might have come first, resulting from negative life events or poor coping strategies that can only be understood at the social level. In this case drugs like Prozac only work to reduce the symptoms of depression temporarily, much like the drug aspirin provides temporary relief from another symptom of stress: headaches.

The following reading describes biological reductionists' attempts to understand autism and schizophrenia. At the social level, these conditions are both characterized by atypical social behavior. Thus, these scientists reason, if the brain areas responsible for social behavior can be identified, then a cure for these problems might be found. One starting point in this strategy is to identify the genes responsible for social behavior. That is exactly what one group of researchers is claiming to have done.

Nicholas Wade*
September 9, 1997

In a stroke of inspired good fortune, biologists have found a gene that turns out to exert profound effects on the social behavior of mice. This is apparently the first gene to be isolated that affects social behavior in mammals, the authors and others say, and it promises to shed light on important disorders of human social behavior like schizophrenia and autism.

Mice that lack the gene look normal and achieve normal grades on tests of learning and memory. But their social behavior is subtly different. They interact with each other less often than do standard mice. They huddle together less, they do not fluff up suitable beds from their nesting material, and they fail to trim one another's whiskers properly. The inattention to barbering is a sign that they do not form the social hierarchy customary among this strain of laboratory mice, in which the dominant mouse trims the whiskers and facial hair of its social inferiors.

"I think this is the first gene to be described that controls social interactions," said Dr. Anthony Wynshaw-Boris, a clinical geneticist at the National Human Genome Research Institute and chief author of the study.

Dr. Richard S. Nowakowski, a neurobiologist at the University of Medicine and Dentistry of New Jersey, said the new finding marked the first time a gene had been found to affect behavior in a mammal. "It is a great leap forward in terms of our thinking about limbic system diseases," he said, referring to schizophrenia and autism, because it "provides molecular clues as to what is going on in these deficits."

The finding was made by means of knock-out mice, animals in which a single gene has been removed or knocked out by genetic engineering. Dr. Wynshaw-Boris and his colleagues decided to knock out the mouse version of a gene discovered in fruit flies, a standard laboratory organism. The gene is called "disheveled" because flies with a mutant version die or develop with disarranged chest hairs and other afflictions.

The disheveled gene is part of a cell-to-cell signaling pathway, one so important that it is found in mice and humans, too, despite the millions of years of evolution that separate mammals from fruit flies. Scanning mouse DNA for genes of similar structure to the fly gene, biologists have found three versions of the gene, known as disheveled 1, 2 and 3.

To learn the gene's role in mice, Dr. Wynshaw-Boris decided to knock out disheveled-1; he expected its absence to make the mice develop abnormally, as do fruit flies that lack the gene. He was surprised to find that the mice looked normal when they grew up. But after colleagues noticed the unusually bushy whiskers of the knock-out mice, a battery of behavioral changes came to light.

One of the most interesting is an inability to screen out extraneous noise and focus on a single stimulus. This symptom, as well as abnormal social behavior, are found in several human psychiatric disorders, like schizophrenia and Tourette's syndrome. Abnormal social behavior is also a feature of autism.

Schizophrenia is thought to have a strong genetic as well as environmental component because the disease is more common than usual among a patient's relatives. From analysis of family pedigrees, epidemiologists have identified several sites on human chromosomes where genes predisposing toward schizophrenia are thought to lie.

Dr. Anne E. Pulver, an epidemiologist who studies schizophrenia at the Johns Hopkins University School of Medicine, said the finding was "really fascinating and needs to be followed up." Although the finding has no immediate relevance to patients, she said, the discovery of genes that predispose toward schizophrenia would help pharmaceutical companies develop drugs, and the mice might be helpful in testing them.

None of the present candidate regions on human chromosomes for genes predisposing toward schizophrenia includes the sites of the human versions of the disheveled genes. But there are probably several more such regions to be found, so the human disheveled genes are not excluded as possible causes of the disease, Dr. Pulver said.

While there are obvious pitfalls in comparing humans with mice, especially in terms of behavior, the two species share a surprising amount in common at the level of their genes.

Whatever its relevance to psychiatry, the new finding has fished out two ends of a very interesting chain, with the disheveled gene at one end and the array of complex behaviors at the other. The connecting links are at present unknown. "We have no idea what the pathways are that go from the beginning to the end," Dr. Wynshaw-Boris said, "or what goes on between the mutation and the social interactions."

The function of the disheveled gene is unknown, other than that its product is one of the first members of an essential communication chain in which a cell signals its neighbor. In the fruit fly this communication system, called the wingless pathway, is used to organize the cells of the developing embryo so that each segment of the fly knows its head from its tail.

When a good system has evolved, nature often adapts it to other uses, and it may be that the wingless pathway has been assigned a role in the adult mammalian brain as well as in development. In the mouse the three disheveled genes are known to be switched on during development of the embryo, and disheveled-1 is also active in the adult mouse, particularly in two regions of the brain known as the cerebellum and hippocampus.

In mice lacking the disheveled-1 gene, the wingless pathway is presumably at risk of complete shutdown since a critical component is missing. Dr. Wynshaw-Boris suggests that in his knock-out mice, the disheveled-2 and disheveled-3 genes can compensate for the lack of disheveled-1 during development, which is why the mice appear normal but cannot remedy the lack of disheveled-1 in the brain.

Dr. Wynshaw-Boris said he had not yet shown his mice to psychiatrists, who might confirm parallels with disordered patients, nor had he given them antipsychotic drugs to see if their symptoms would abate.

Questions

1. What was the first clue that the mice were affected by the knock-out procedure?
2. What kinds of behavior are thought to be controlled by the limbic system?
3. In what areas of the brain are the disheveled genes active in adult mice? What are these areas thought to control? What types of symptoms might we expect if these areas fail to function normally?
4. What evidence suggests that this discovery may eventually help people with schizophrenia? What evidence suggests that the disheveled genes have little or nothing to do with schizophrenia?
5. What are the advantages of using laboratory mice to study human brain systems? What are the greatest dangers of this type of research? Do you think it is ethically or morally acceptable to do the kinds of studies reported here?

Section II
Cognition and Consciousness

Reading 6

Evolutionary Necessity or Glorious Accident?

Introduction

Consciousness is a puzzling phenomenon. The fact that you are almost always consciously aware of yourself and your environment may not seem puzzling to you, but trying to explain the mechanisms and functions of this awareness is one of the most contentious issues in psychology. Psychologists are only beginning to understand such basic questions as how information gets into our consciousness, what neural structures are involved, and what purposes—if any—all of this serves. This next reading focuses on the third of these questions.

Taking an evolutionary perspective, the scientists in this reading wonder what adaptive advantages consciousness might provide and what selective pressures might have caused it to come about. As the title of this article implies, views about consciousness can be divided roughly into two camps: those that see it as serving some purpose (as an "evolutionary necessity") and those that see it as serving no purpose at all (as a "glorious accident").

Of particular interest in this reading is conscious awareness of ourselves. Although psychologists and biologists working in this area cannot even agree on how to define or measure self-awareness, they are not deterred. And the data and theory they are generating are beginning to help us better understand the puzzle of self-awareness.

Natalie Angier*
April 22, 1997

The self is like an irritating television jingle: you cannot get it out of your head. Whatever you do on this blue planet with your allotted three score and ten, whatever you taste, embrace, learn or create, all will be filtered through the self. Even sleep offers no escape, for who is it that struts through the center of every dream but you, yourself and id?

Call it self-awareness, self-identity, mind, consciousness, or even soul, but the sense of self, of being a particular individual set apart from others, seems intrinsic to the human condition. After all, Homo sapiens have large brains, and they are awfully good at taking stock of their surroundings. Sooner or later, they were bound to notice themselves, and the impermeable physical barrier between themselves and others. The invention of personal pronouns, philosophy and large-pore illuminating mirrors was bound to follow.

Yet as natural and inevitable as human self-awareness may seem, evolutionary biologists and psychologists do not take its existence for granted. Instead, they are asking deceptively simple questions that cut to the core of selfhood. Among them: What good is the self, anyway? Has self-awareness been selected by evolutionary pressures, or is it, to borrow a phrase from Stephen Jay Gould, a "glorious accident," the byproduct of a large intelligence that allows humans to build tools and otherwise manipulate their environment? Might humans not fare just as well operating like computers, which, cyberfantasy notwithstanding, do their jobs without mulling over why they are here?

The quest to understand the evolution of the self is part of the much larger and very fashionable study of consciousness, which has spawned enough scientific symposiums, Web sites and books to render even the most diligent student unconscious. But most consciousness research focuses on so-called proximate mechanisms, the question of how the brain knows itself and which neural pathways and patterns of synaptic firings might underlie self-awareness. Evolutionary researchers concern themselves with ultimate mechanisms, the whys and wherefores of self. They are taking a phylogenetic approach, seeking to understand when self-awareness arose in the evolutionary past, whether other species have a sense of self, and if so, how it can be demonstrated.

The researchers are aided in their efforts by recent advances in the study of infants, and improved tools for asking questions of subjects that lack language skills. The new work indicates that an infant's sense of self, once thought to develop only gradually over the first couple of years of life, may arise prenatally. Those insights, in turn, suggest that self-awareness is not limited to the species capable of growling, "I want to be alone."

A number of biologists now suspect that a robustly articulated sense of self, far from being an afterthought of abundant cortical tissue, is very much

*Reprinted with permission from *The New York Times.*

the point of the human brain. They propose that consciousness allows humans to manipulate the most important resource of all—themselves—and to use the invented self as a tool to advance their own interests among their peers. This theory, in turn, suggests that the sense of self, of being set apart like an island afloat in a dark cosmic sea, paradoxically may have arisen because humans evolved in a highly interdependent group—because, in fact, no human is an island.

The rudiments of selfhood are as ancient as the plasma membrane, the greasy coating that separates one single-celled organism from another. "Even something as simple as an amoeba has a boundary between the self and the outside world," said Dr. David Darling, a former computer researcher and author of "Soul Search" (Villard Books, 1995) about the nature of self-consciousness. "That physical and chemical border is the beginning of some kind of self." Most creatures are sufficiently self-aware to place themselves first on their list. "It would be unlikely for an insect to start grooming a neighbor's foot," said Dr. May R. Berenbaum, an entomologist at the University of Illinois in Urbana-Champaign and author of "Bugs in the System" (Addison-Wesley, 1995). "You wouldn't want to waste energy promoting the well-being of somebody else."

But it is one thing to have a foot-jerk preference for No. 1, and another to be conscious of that preference, or to have some sense of the self's relationship to others. Dr. Stephen W. Porges, a neurobiology researcher at the University of Maryland in College Park, defines a sense of self as essentially self-actualization, of acting upon the world rather than being acted on. He sees the emergence of self-awareness reflected in the neuroanatomical differences between the reptilian and mammalian brains. Reptile are sit-and-wait feeders, he explains, and their primary neural structures, the brainstem and hypothalamus, are driven by their viscera. "When there's food available, they eat," Dr. Porges said. "When there isn't, their brain reduces their metabolic demands and slows everything up." Moreover, reptiles must react defensively to fine-tune their physiology; for example, by moving into the shade to cool themselves, or into the sun for warmth. For the cold-bloods, Dr. Porges said, life is a perpetual case of matter over mind, and there is no room for mindfulness.

Mammals, by comparison, are dynamic foragers and explorers of their environment. Regardless of external circumstances, their core body temperature and metabolism are maintained stably by the brainstem and hypothalamus, thus freeing up neural circuits to permit an active as opposed to reactive stance in the world. With the development of the cortex, mammals, particularly primates, gained the ability to engage with others, vocalize, display facial expressions and otherwise show evidence of emotions, all of which Dr. Porges counts as aspects of self-awareness.

In describing the transition from the reptilian to the primate brain, Dr. Porges uses the metaphor of emergence from the Garden of Eden. "In the garden, food is available, but there is no awareness of self," he said. "When we leave the garden, we must search for food, and we are aware of self. That is the forbidden knowledge."

Many mammals give signs that they know themselves, at least well enough to know their place. A spotted hyena, for example, learns shortly after birth where it stands in the hierarchy of its clan, a position determined by its mother's status, and it behaves accordingly, bullying its subordinates and groveling up to its superiors. Yet many researchers are reluctant to attribute that sort of bureaucratic behavior to genuine consciousness. They seek evidence that an animal is aware of its individuality—that it has an internal life.

One classic method for testing an animal's degree of self-awareness is the mirror self-recognition test, which has been mainly used in primate studies. In the experiment, a researcher sees how an animal reacts when confronted with its image in a mirror, and whether it recognizes that, for example, a bit of paint has been daubed on its face.

The initial results of such tests seemed to indicate an intellectual divide between the monkeys and the great apes, the primate group most closely related to humans, which includes chimpanzees, gorillas and orangutans. Apes were said to be able to recognize themselves in the mirror, while monkeys were not, supposed evidence that only apes have self-awareness. But recently, Dr. Marc D. Hauser, an associate professor of psychology and anthropology at Harvard University and his colleagues showed that cotton-top tamarins, a South American monkey, can indeed recognize themselves in the mirror, staring in fascination after their shock of white hair had been dyed a punkish neon color. Yet Dr. Hauser and others dispute whether the results of this or any other mirror test are all that revealing. "The mirror test is not the be-all and end-all of self-recognition," he said. "People have been relying on it too much. What we need are a battery of tests to look at many aspects of self-awareness."

To that end, Dr. Hauser has lately borrowed a page from child development studies and begun subjecting nonhuman primates to the so-called false-belief test, a measure of how well one individual can appreciate that another individual might have a mental geography that differs from one's own. In a hypothetical example of such tests, three monkeys might be allowed to watch a trainer put a banana into a box. Two of the monkeys are then taken away, just long enough for the remaining monkey to see the trainer moving the banana from the box to a basket. Dr. Hauser's question: when its two fellows are returned to the training area, will the observing monkey show signs that it recognizes they now hold a false belief about the banana's location? Preliminary results with tamarins suggest that the monkeys do have something approaching a theory of mind: the observing monkey will look at the box seemingly in full expectation that the fooled monkeys will hunt for the banana there.

In this regard, at least, nonhuman primates seem to be like 3-year-old children, who show with their eye gaze that they, too, recognize another's false belief. Interestingly, though, when 3-year-olds are asked, as in the above example, where the benighted individuals will look, they say, "The basket." "Their eyes look at the right place, but they can't yet express their awareness of the deception," Dr. Hauser said. "They have implicit rather than explicit knowledge." By 4, the children make the correct response with language as well as with eye gaze.

Assuming that some nonhuman species have an implicit self-awareness, researchers expect that such intelligence is likely to be limited to, or at least most prominent in, highly social animals like primates, and possibly dolphins and a sprinkling of others. All research points to the importance of the group in giving birth to the self, and nowhere is the link more clearly seen than in humans. "Even before a baby is born, it has an identity, a place in the social hierarchy," said Dr. Roy F. Baumeister, a professor of psychology at Case Western Reserve University in Cleveland. "It may be given a name, a Social Security number, even a bank account, long before it has consciousness." The earliest contents of self-description are categorical ones, Dr. Baumeister said. By the age of 15 months or so, children identify themselves by their family, their sex and the fact that they are children rather than adults.

Dr. Alan Fogel of the University of Utah in Salt Lake City, who studies the development of the self in children, proposes that an infant first understands itself relationally, by registering its impact on others. Contrary to old notions that a young baby knows no distinction between itself and its mother, he said, recent work suggests that even newborns can tell the difference between when they move or touch themselves and when they are being moved or touched by others.

Dr. Fogel has found that babies see themselves as part of a "relational field," which they can alter with their behavior. For example, he said, if a mother smiles and coos at a 2-month-old, the baby will smile and gurgle in response, a seamless exchange of delight. But if the mother suddenly turns stony-faced, the baby will stop, turn away and then look back with a smile, as though trying to reinitiate the exchange. If that fails, the baby eventually turns away, apparently dejected.

"Some people argue that, well, it is just because the baby's expectations were upset," Dr. Fogel said. "But I argue that the baby has a sense of itself and its role in the relationship, as shown by that fact that the baby tries to reestablish communication. It doesn't wither away and do nothing at all."

In seeing itself as dependent on yet distinct from the mother, and in seeking to manipulate the relationship with its behavior, a baby demonstrates, on a small scale, the benefits of self-awareness and offers insight into why humans are so full of themselves. Dr. Steven Pinker, professor of cognitive science at the Massachusetts Institute of Technology and author of "How the Mind Works," a book to be published this fall by W. W. Norton, points out that humans are the most elaborately social of all species, possibly as a result of environmental conditions pitting early humans against other hominids and apes. Self-awareness helps an individual maximize the benefits that he or she can reap from the group.

"Our fate depends on what other people think of us," Dr. Pinker said. "It would make sense to apply our intelligence to assuring that social interactions come out in our favor."

For example, he said, people want to form alliances with those they deem brave, honest and trustworthy. "Its to our advantage to be seen as brave, trustworthy, kind and so forth," Dr. Pinker said. "We have the ability to float above ourselves and look down at ourselves, to play back tapes of our own behavior to evaluate and manipulate it. Knowing thyself is a way of making thyself as palatable as possible to others."

Certain oddities of self-awareness support the theory that it has adaptive value, Dr. Pinker said. Self-deception is one of them. As psychology tests reveal, most people have a slightly inflated image of themselves and their talents. "There may be an advantage to believing that one is kinder, smarter and more in control than you really are," he said. "To the extent that all of us are at least occasional liars, the best liar is one who believes his own lies." Those with low self-esteem, then, may be the most truthful members of the tribe, but somehow that sort of honesty will not win you allies or a date on Saturday night.

QUESTIONS

1. How do proximate studies of consciousness differ from ultimate studies of consciousness? Which approach is most represented in this reading?
2. How does Dr. Porges define "self-awareness"? How does this compare with the definitions of "consciousness" you have or have discussed in class?
3. In the traditional mirror task, an animal looking into a mirror sees that the animal in the mirror has a red dot on its face. If that animal correctly recognizes that the red dot is on its own face (i.e., recognizes that the face in the mirror is its own face), it is said to have self-awareness. Do you agree this is a valid measure?
4. In Hauser's adaptation of the mirror test, tamarins looking into a mirror see the tamarin in the mirror has unnatural neon-colored hair instead of the normal white hair. Tamarins stare at this image in the mirror longer than they do when their hair has not been dyed, suggesting to Hauser that tamarins have self-awareness. Do you agree this is a valid measure?
5. Many of the people interviewed in this article argue that evolving in a social environment is important for the development of self-awareness. What arguments do they make in support of this position? Which do you find the most and the least convincing?

Reading 7

Was Freud Wrong?
Are Dreams the Brain's Start-up Test?

Introduction

Freud's theory of dreams has a special place in psychoanalysis: The first book ever published on psychoanalytic theory was Freud's The Interpretation of Dreams. *In it he outlined his belief that unconscious desires and conflicts try to get into consciousness during the night but our ego protects us by transforming the true images of the conflict (the latent content of the dream) into different images that are related but unrecognizable (the manifest content of the dream). Because dream images are related to our unconscious conflicts, dreams are the key to unlocking the unconscious mind.*

Although Freud's ideas about dreams remain popular among the general public, they have increasingly lost favor among psychologists. We have learned a great deal about dreams in the 100 years since the publication of The Interpretation of Dreams, *and often what we learn is inconsistent with Freudian notions. For example, the idea that dreams occur when we have unresolved conflict seems to be contradicted by the finding that all adults dream about the same amount every night (even though unconscious conflict varies a great deal from person to person and from day to day) and that all infants and almost all mammals dream too (what unconscious conflicts are mice and 1-week-old humans dealing with?). The following article further challenges the Freudian theory of dreams. Research has now identified why dreams often seem incoherent and disorganized; this new evidence seems contradictory to Freud's explanation of latent content being hidden beneath a layer of manifest content.*

Nicholas Wade*
January 6, 1998

New measurements taken from sleeping people explain, at least in part, why dreams tend to have such bizarre but vivid story lines.

The findings deal a blow to the Freudian interpretation of dreams but leave open the possibility that some useful personal meaning can be extracted from them. The main purpose of dreams, however, the authors of the new study believe, is to test whether the brain has had enough sleep and, if so, to wake it up.

The new results, based on a method of scanning the activity of the living brain, show that in sleep, the frontal lobes of the brain are shut down. In the absence of activity in those lobes, which integrate other information and make sense of the outside world, the sleeping brain's images are driven by its emotional centers. The content of these dreams may be vivid and gripping but lacks coherence.

"The feeling in dreams that you don't know where you are, you can't think straight and you can't direct the action, is extremely consonant with these results," said Dr. J. Allan Hobson, an expert on dreams at the Harvard Medical School.

The new results are consistent with the theory that memories are consolidated during sleep. From the pattern of activity that was recorded, "it seems that memories already in system are being read out and filed in terms of their emotional salience, which is an extremely interesting idea," Dr. Hobson said.

The new measurements were made by a team led by Dr. Allen R. Braun of the National Institutes of Health and Dr. Thomas J. Balkin of the Walter Reed Army Institute of Research and are reported in the current issue of *Science*.

They applied the technique known as PET scanning to sleeping subjects. In a PET scan, an injection of mildly radioactive glucose is used to visualize changes in blood flow to the brain. Since actively firing nerve cells need more blood, PET scans show the working regions of the brain lighting up, while passive areas remain dark.

The two biologists focused on the two forms of sleep, known as slow-wave sleep and REM sleep. REM sleep, so named because of the rapid eyeball movements that occur then, takes place about four times during the night and is the phase from which the most vivid dreams are recalled.

A longstanding puzzle of REM sleep is that the brain appears to be just as active as when a person is awake, as judged by measuring the brain's electrical waves at the surface of the scalp, yet it is completely unresponsive to

---

the outside world. Dr. Braun and Dr. Balkin say they have found an explanation: during REM sleep, the primary visual cortex is shut down, along with other input areas that relay information from the senses. The primary visual cortex is the area in the back of the head where information from the eyes first reaches the cortex. The sleeping brain is thus cut off from its usual stream of information from the outside world.

Also off line during REM sleep are the brain's frontal lobes. These include many of the higher centers of thought and action, including working memory, the planning and executive function, and the centers that integrate data from other regions of the brain. Much of the rest of the brain, including the centers that handle emotions and the laying down of long-term memories, are highly active during REM sleep.

"The frontal lobes are involved in working memory, which keep data on line for immediate reference, so if these areas are shut down during REM sleep, it might account for the fact that in dreams, the plot doesn't unfold in linear sequence, and the identities of different individuals morph into each other," Dr. Braun said.

Striking as dreams are to the dreamer, however, he and Dr. Balkin believe that the principal purpose of the activity seen during REM sleep is to test whether the various working centers of the brain have completed whatever the restorative process is that presumably takes place during sleep. This testing process occurs several times during the night. When the restoration is judged to be complete, the brain is made to wake up. "Dreams are probably not necessary, they are just an epiphenomenon that occurs during the testing phase," Dr. Balkin said.

Dr. Hobson said many people had assumed that REM sleep was a kind of test program "but it's got to be more than that."

A common idea is that memories are consolidated during sleep. Working memory is not available because the frontal lobes are closed down, which may be why dreams themselves are not remembered. But memories already laid down seem to be replayed during sleep, as has been shown by experiments in rats. Dr. Braun and Dr. Balkin say their findings are compatible with this idea, too, since they find the hippocampus, a region where memories are processed for long storage elsewhere, is among the regions activated during REM sleep.

But their finding that the brain's higher centers are shut down during sleep is not helpful to psychoanalytic theory. "Freud postulated that dream content had to be monitored, with wishes being screened as they emerged from the unconscious," Dr. Braun said. "But for that, the prefrontal cortex would have to be on line."

Still, dreams may reflect the brain's activity in some significant way. Dr. Balkin said, "It doesn't mean that dreams are meaningless, but they are not useful, as in working through unresolved conflicts, as Freud thought."

QUESTIONS

1. How do Braun and his colleagues explain the tendency of dreams to be incoherent and nonlinear? What evidence supports this position?
2. According to the research cited here, is it more likely that you would be aware of visual stimuli (e.g., lights) or an auditory stimuli (e.g., noise) during REM sleep?
3. What aspects of the memory-consolidation theory of dreams is supported by this new data?
4. What aspects of Freud's theory of dreams seem inconsistent with this data?
5. Are any aspects of Freud's theory supported by this data?

Reading 8

Getting to the Truth in Child Abuse Cases: New Methods

Introduction

Research on human memory often turns up surprising and counterintuitive findings. For example, most people cannot remember anything that happened to them before they were 3 years old. People who think they have very early childhood memories are often wrong; very likely they do not remember the actual event but instead heard the story so many times as a child that they reconstructed a new memory in childhood. This explanation may seem very odd to you, especially if you believe you have an early childhood memory. But as you will see in this next reading, children's memories are not always accurate. What they think is a genuine memory of an actual event as it happened to them can in fact be a created (or reconstructed) memory, reconstructed from stories they were told or even questions they were asked.

The problem of distinguishing between real and reconstructed childhood memories is usually not of great importance. But what if the memory in question is one of physical or sexual abuse? Then it would be of the greatest importance to know whether the memory was genuine. Just this scenario began occurring regularly in the 1980s, resulting in a series of highly publicized trials. Although each case was unique, many fit the following pattern: Parents are suspicious of abuse at a day care, children are questioned and at first deny abuse, after repeated questioning some children change their story to admit abuse, more children change their story, although no physical evidence of abuse is found, a conviction is obtained on the strength of the children's testimony. In 1980 few suspected that children's memories of abuse could possibly be other than genuine. But the more than 500 studies conducted since then have convinced most experts that in certain circumstances some children reconstruct vivid memories of being sexually abused, when in fact they never were.

CAREY GOLDBERG*
SEPTEMBER 8, 1998

After more than 12 years in prison, convicted of raping children at his family's suburban Boston day care center despite his avowals of innocence, Gerald Amirault says he is pinning his hopes on new science to get him out.

Not on microbiology; not on DNA testing. No physical evidence of that sort exists against Mr. Amirault, his sister and their late mother. All three were convicted in 1986 and 1987 in the Fells Acres Day School case, which has become the longest-running of the highly publicized day care sexual abuse cases that swept the country back then.

Rather, Mr. Amirault is counting on the science of psychology. And judging by a blistering ruling this summer in his sister's legal battle, he may have a shot.

Those day care cases, it turns out, from the McMartin Preschool in California to Wee Care in New Jersey, set off an explosion of psychological research into the accuracy of children's memories and reporting of events.

In the last decade, researchers estimate, 500 studies have been conducted on children's "suggestibility"—the extent to which suggestions implanted by adult interviewers can influence children's recollections and accounts.

Though debate still burns high on some points—like the general level of children's accuracy and how resistant they are to disclosing that they have been abused—researchers describe an emerging consensus over how children should be interviewed to minimize false reports. Warring camps of psychologists also appear to have reached broad agreement on this basic picture: The vast majority of the tens of thousands of child sexual abuse accusations each year are true, and most children display a tremendous capacity to be accurate; but under certain conditions, if they are pushed and prodded in the wrong ways, children may say false things. And preschoolers of 3 and 4 tend to be more suggestible than older children.

It was that body of research that underlay the Massachusetts Superior Court ruling by Judge Isaac Borenstein in June that Mr. Amirault's sister, Cheryl Amirault LeFave, should be granted a new trial on her conviction of sexual abuse because of new scientific findings.

"Overzealous and inadequately trained investigators, perhaps unaware of the grave dangers of using improper interviewing and investigative techniques,

---

questioned these children and their parents in a climate of panic, if not hysteria, creating a highly prejudicial and irreparable set of mistakes," the judge wrote. "These grave errors led to the testimony of the children being forever tainted."

Prosecutors maintain that the Amiraults got fair trials, and the state supreme court has repeatedly ruled against the family. But the court has never dealt with a lower court ruling like Judge Borenstein's.

Judges elsewhere, however, have previously cited suggestibility research in overturning a ruling made when it was all but given among clinicians—based more on gut instinct than data—that children would never lie about sexual abuse. The research played a role in a New Jersey appeals court's 1993 decision to free Margaret Kelly Michaels, who was convicted in 1988 in the Wee Care case, and has figured in other rulings and verdicts. The Michaels decision noted that "certain questions planted sexual information in the children's minds." The developing consensus has been emerging in guidelines set by associations of psychiatrists, psychologists and other professionals who deal with accusations of child sexual abuse. Among the rules of thumb are these:

- Children should be interviewed in the most open-ended way possible at first, allowed to engage in "free recall" rather than responding to specific questions. For example, in its 1997 guidelines for evaluating children who may have been abused, the American Academy of Child and Adolescent Psychiatry recommends that interviewers' initial questions should not be "leading or suggestive and should be phrased in such a way that an inability to recall or lack of knowledge is acceptable. A leading question is, 'Uncle Joe touched your bottom, didn't he?' A suggestive question is: 'Did Uncle Joe touch your bottom?' "
- The interviewers should be as unbiased as possible about whether abuse actually occurred, because studies have shown that interviewer bias can influence responses from children eager to please adults.
- No bribes, threats or peer pressure should be brought to bear on the children. There should be no "Johnny told me. Why won't you?"
- The number of interviews, repetitious questions and leading questions should be kept to a minimum. Many communities around the country, including virtually every major city, have set up children's assessment centers over the last several years so that children who may have been abused can undergo one-stop interviews.
- Interviews should be carefully documented and preserved so the record can be checked for tainting.
- Children should not be encouraged to imagine acts that did not occur. Such imaginings, studies have shown, can sometimes be confused with real memories.
- "Anatomically detailed" dolls, dolls with genitalia meant to help children demonstrate the abuse perpetrated on them, should be used with great care if at all. Research has shown that a child's natural interest in the dolls' sexual organs can sometimes mislead, though the dolls are also known to help children disclose abuse. The American Professional Society on the Abuse

> of Children's guidelines say: "Anatomical dolls should not be used as a diagnostic test for sexual abuse."

The evolution of a consensus about child suggestibility has carried particular scientific drama because of the high stakes involved: Underestimate the power of suggestibility and innocent people could go to jail; overestimate it, and abused children might not be believed, traumatizing them still more and allowing child abusers to victimize more children.

Worries that abuse is underreported have been bolstered by suggestibility studies showing that children are likelier to lie by denying something although it really happened than by making something up that never occurred, noted Dr. Carolyn Newberger, an expert on sexual abuse at Harvard Medical School.

"That would indicate there are far more children who are abused and don't let anyone know than who are not abused and tell someone they are," Dr. Newberger said.

Yet getting children to say they have been hurt is critical, because diagnosing sexual abuse can still be difficult. The American Academy of Child and Adolescent Psychiatry guidelines note that studies have shown that no one symptom characterizes a majority of sexually abused children, and about one-third of victims exhibit no symptoms.

What researchers have done, then, is to close in on sexual abuse by creating or exploiting situations like it, as well as conditions and strategies that mimic those of forensic interviews, then building a case and plugging holes, in study after study.

"I'm not saying they're the perfect analogue of sex abuse, but you look at research as a building process," said Dr. Stephen Ceci, a Cornell University developmental psychologist who has been a leader of the camp of researchers who emphasize how suggestible children are.

"Each new study tries to rule out some weakness in the prior studies," Dr. Ceci said. "People looked at painful things, embarrassing things, genital things, within a whole web of motives: lying to protect loved ones; lying to avoid embarrassment; lying to gain material reward; lying to avoid punishment; lying to keep secrets; lying to sustain a game."

Suggestibility studies once focused largely on asking a misleading question and seeing how it affected children's perceptions of an event they had witnessed. Now, many studies have moved toward focusing more on personally salient events, in situations more reminiscent of abuse.

In an affidavit for Ms. LeFave's motion for a new trial, Dr. Maggie Bruck of McGill University, another top researcher in Dr. Ceci's camp, cited a 1996 study from the Monographs of the Society for Research in Child Development. The researchers, Margaret S. Steward and David S. Steward, interviewed children using anatomical dolls three times after a pediatric clinic visit. "With each interview, children's false reports of anal touching increased,"

Dr. Bruck wrote. "By the final interview, which took place six months after the initial visit, more than one-third of the children falsely reported anal touching."

But other studies by Dr. Gail Goodman, a University of California at Davis psychologist and a foremost suggestibility researcher in the camp that tends to emphasize children's truthfulness, highlighted the great accuracy of children's reports even in intimate situations. Dr. Goodman and colleagues studied the accounts of children who had been catheterized for a necessary test of the urinary tract that the researchers considered the closest medical procedure to child abuse—embarrassing, genital and painful.

"What we've done that's somewhat different from what Ceci usually does is we ask very abuse-related questions," she said. "He asks, did they tear up the teddy bear and spill coffee on you? And we ask, didn't he touch your bottom or, how many times did he kiss you?"

"We find," she said, "that once the kids are around 5 years of age, they're just surprisingly accurate on those kinds of questions. The 3-year-olds tend to make more like 25 percent errors on average."

Researchers say the focus is also shifting to the individual differences that make one child much more suggestible than another, and to experimental interviewing techniques that help children tell more without contaminating their memories.

If there is one other great point of consensus among child-abuse experts, it is on the great need for even more training of social workers, police investigators, psychologists and others in the proper way to deal with children who may have been abused.

"Consensus about what people say they should do shouldn't be confused with what's actually happening," said Dr. Michael E. Lamb, a researcher at the National Institute of Child Health and Human Development in Bethesda, Md. "We've found that in fact, in the field, the overwhelming majority of the questions put to children during investigative interviews are more focused questions and only between 2 and 6 percent are actually open-ended."

True to Dr. Lamb's findings, cases are still cropping up in which highly questionable interviewing techniques have been used. The Washington branch of the American Civil Liberties Union has complained that in the 1994 Wenatchee sex-ring case in Washington State, the police investigation violated several basic tenets of interviewing; among them, children were threatened with punishment or marathon interrogation if they did not say that they had been sexually abused.

As for Gerald Amirault, he is serving his 30- to 40-year prison sentence and watching what happens as prosecutors appeal the ruling in his sister's case to the Massachusetts Supreme Judicial Court. If the ruling holds, Mr. Amirault can try a similar appeal, said his lawyer, Daniel R. Williams of Manhattan.

When he was on trial in 1986, Mr. Amirault said, "It was looked at as right to question the children the way they did."

But back then, he noted, suggestibility research "was a brand new area, a brand spanking new area. The expert pool hadn't even been established. So I couldn't even find experts."

Now, "The way you perceive everything is looked at in a totally different light," he said. "I would love to go back to trial."

Questions

1. On what points do psychologists agree concerning children's reports of sexual abuse? On what points are there still debate?
2. Give an example of a leading question. Rephrase the question to fit with guidelines set by the American Academy of Child and Adolescent Psychiatry (AACAP).
3. Why might the AACAP argue against repeated questioning of child witnesses? What aspect of human memory makes this practice dangerous?
4. What AACAP guideline did Washington police violate in the 1994 Wenatchee sex-ring case? Why do we suspect this technique to bias children's testimony more than an adult's?
5. Ceci's research shows that children's memory can be inaccurate; Goodman's shows that children's memory can be quite accurate. What conclusions would you draw given that research supports both positions? How suspicious of a child's testimony would you be if you had to serve on a jury of such a case?

Reading 9

I.Q. Scores Are Up, and Psychologists Wonder Why

Introduction

Intelligence testing has a relatively short, but highly controversial history. Some pioneers of intelligence testing—such as Alfred Binet who introduced an I.Q. test that was later modified into the well-known Stanford-Binet test—were motivated to identify children who lagged behind age-mates in skills necessary to be successful in school. Others, such as Francis Galton, were more interested in using intelligence tests to prove the intellectual and even moral superiority of their own racial group to others. The use of I.Q. tests to argue for racial superiority continues today and can be seen in the publication of The Bell Curve *by Charles Murray and Richard J. Herrnstein. In this book the authors argue that biological differences between the races are the most likely explanation for European Americans' higher I.Q. scores relative to African and Hispanic Americans.*

It is because of this polemical past that even the apparent good news that I.Q. scores seem to be increasing all over the world does not escape contention. If I.Q. tests measure innate ability, how can scores be increasing in a time span too short for natural selection mechanisms? And if I.Q. tests are influenced by culture and education, why are they increasing in almost every culture? To make matters more complex, performance on achievement tests such as the SAT have declined dramatically over the same time period that witnessed sharp increases in I.Q. test scores. This complex pattern leaves plenty of room for different interpretations. And as might be expected from a research area used to heated debate, psychologists are far from agreeing on how best to interpret the current trend in I.Q. scores.

Trish Hall*
February 24, 1998

It is a favorite pastime of older people to lament the defects of the young. Every generation seems to be convinced that in its day, standards were higher, schools were tougher and kids were smarter.

But if I.Q. scores are any measure, and even their critics agree they measure something, people are getting smarter. Researchers who study intelligence say scores around the world have been increasing so fast that a high proportion of people regarded as normal at the turn of the century would be considered way below average by today's tests.

Psychologists offer a variety of possible explanations for the increase, including better nutrition, urbanization, more experience with test taking, and smaller families. Some even say that television and video games have made children's brains more agile.

But no explanation is without its critics, and no one can say with certainty what effects, if any, the change is having on how people lead their daily lives. It is all the more mysterious because it seems to be happening in the absence of a simultaneous increase in scores on achievement tests.

One explanation for the rise is ruled out: heredity. Because the increase has taken place in a relatively short period of time, it cannot be due to genetic factors. In fact, some experts say, the changing test scores show intelligence is much more flexible and more subject to environmental influences than anyone thought. "Everyone is getting smarter in some way, and a lot smarter," said Dr. Ulrich Neisser, a psychology professor at Cornell University.

"We're living in a golden age," he said. "Look at all the technological advances, at a rate that it's impossible to grasp, even. We couldn't have done this with the intellectual skills people had in the 19th century."

The worldwide pattern of rising scores in industrialized nations was discovered by Dr. James R. Flynn, originally from the United States and now a professor emeritus of political studies at the University of Otago in Dunedin, New Zealand. He began looking into the subject in the 1980's in an effort to rebut Dr. Arthur Jensen, the professor from the University of California at Berkeley who argued that even if the environments of blacks and whites were equalized, the 15-point gap in I.Q. scores between the races would only be partly eliminated.

As Dr. Flynn investigated, he found that I.Q. scores were going up almost everywhere he looked. "Kids obviously are going in there with a skill that causes better performance," he said. "What we've got to do is find the real-world analogue of test skills that are escalating."

What these skills might be is unclear, especially given the fact that scores on the Scholastic Aptitude Test declined from the mid-1960's until

---

*Reprinted with permission from *The New York Times*.

the early 1980's. "I expect it's some type of abstract problem solving skill," Dr. Flynn said.

Other researchers have confirmed Dr. Flynn's findings, and Dr. Neisser, who ran a seminar on the phenomenon in 1996, is editing a book on the subject. The book, "The Rising Curve: Long-Term Gains in I.Q. and Related Measures," is to be published this spring by the American Psychological Association.

Dr. Neisser sees his book as a rebuttal to the 1994 book by Charles Murray and Richard J. Herrnstein, "The Bell Curve," which argued that there is a strong link between I.Q. and income, and consequently, class and upward mobility. It noted the increase in I.Q. scores, but it did not see the upward movement as inconsistent with its thesis.

In an interview, Mr. Murray said that despite the increase, a 15-point gap between blacks and whites on I.Q. tests remains.

Although the gap remains, Dr. Flynn, who in the early 1960's worked for the Congress of Racial Equality in Kentucky, said the movement in scores suggests that the gap need not be permanent. If blacks in 1995 had the same mean I.Q. that whites had in 1945, he said, it may be that the average black environment of 1995 was equivalent in quality to the average white environment of 1945. "Is that really so implausible?" Dr. Flynn asked.

Although I.Q. tests have been given for many decades, the steady rise in scores was not apparent because the tests are regularly adjusted, or renormed, so that half the people score below 100 and half score above, regardless of how many questions are answered correctly.

Dr. Flynn discovered the rise in test scores by studying results of tests that have been unchanged (and unpublished) over decades, such as those used by the military, and by examining studies of people who took two versions of a given I.Q. test, the current one, and a forthcoming replacement. Nearly always, people scored higher on the old test.

Most of his work was done on tests from urban, industrialized countries. While he said there are indications of similar gains on I.Q. in urban areas of less developed countries, such as Brazil and China, the data are not considered as good.

The largest gains were found on Raven's Progressive Matrices, which were first published in 1938 by John C. Raven and developed to measure abstract reasoning ability. By relying on shapes rather than words, the widely used tests are supposed to be impervious to the influence of culture and education.

On Raven's, he found that scores were growing an average of six points per decade in the industrialized countries. The rise is quite startling when applied to real people. For instance, someone in the late 19th century who scored in the 90th percentile on Raven's—or higher than 90 percent of those who took the test—would score at only the fifth percentile on today's test, Dr. Neisser said.

Dr. Flynn also studied other widely used intelligence tests, such as the Stanford-Binet and the various Wechsler Scales, such as the Wechsler Intelligence Scale for Children. He looked at data from 73 studies with 7,500 subjects and found that between 1932 and 1978, whites in the United States gained 14 points on the various Wechsler and Binet tests.

If a representative sample of today's children took the Stanford-Binet test used in 1932, about a quarter of them would be defined as very superior, a rating usually accorded to fewer than 3 percent of the population, Dr. Neisser said.

Although the Stanford-Binet and Wechsler increases were smaller than those on Raven's, Dr. Flynn found that the jumps would have been similar if he had considered only the sections on Stanford-Binet and Wechsler measuring abstract reasoning skills, meant to assess pure intelligence, unaffected by education. The increases were far smaller or nonexistent for sections of the tests that reflected skills learned in school.

Dr. Wendy M. Williams, a professor in the department of human development at Cornell and one of the contributors to "The Rising Curve," said that fluid intelligence, or the ability to know how to do something, is growing while crystallized intelligence, the possession of information, is decreasing. As a result, she said, children from the 1930's who would do badly on Raven's compared with today's students would probably far outperform the current crop on questions like "What is the boiling point of water?"

Just as a number of factors may contribute to the lack of knowledge children have—fewer classroom hours, less challenging textbooks—a number, too, might contribute to higher I.Q. scores. For instance, she said, children today encounter mazes and puzzles on the bags that come with fast food, on the place mats in restaurants, and on the backs of cereal boxes. These games appear in almost identical format on I.Q. tests. Indeed, she said, a maze used on a place mat at the International House of Pancakes is identical to one used on a Wechsler test.

The kinds of intelligence that are promoted and respected vary from time to time, said Dr. Patricia Greenfield, a psychology professor at the University of California at Los Angeles, who has contributed a chapter to "The Rising Curve." Playing computer games like Tetris promotes very different skills from reading novels. "People who think of people who read and write well as intelligent people would feel intelligence has gone down," she said. "That's very common. It's nostalgia for old media and the forms of intelligence they develop."

The new skills, she said, are manifested in the world. "Flynn will tell you we don't have more Mozarts and Beethovens," Dr. Greenfield said. "I say, look at the achievements of science, like DNA. The double helix is a very visual thing. Or look at all the technological developments of this century.

"Maybe in prior centuries they had more classical music composers, but there were fewer scientific breakthroughs. It's culture specific. The forms of intelligence are changing."

Questions

1. Between 1932 and 1978, how much have scores on the Wechsler and Binet increased?
2. Scores on the SAT have decreased dramatically over the past decades. Can Williams's distinction between fluid and crystal intelligence explain how this could happen while I.Q. scores have increased?
3. Why does Flynn's finding that I.Q. scores are increasing worldwide argue against Jensen's claim that racial differences in intelligence are genetic?
4. Raven's Progressive Matrices task was designed to measure native intelligence impervious to culture or education. How can we explain the sharp rise in scores on this test over the past 60 years?
5. What stance does Greenfield (at the end of the article) take on the question of whether intelligence is increasing or decreasing? How does this view differ from that expressed by Neisser (near the beginning of the article)? With which position do you agree?

Reading 10

Intelligence in All Its Interactive Aspects

Introduction

What do you mean about a person when you say they are "smart"? Do you mean they are good at math, or have a prodigious vocabulary, or are quick-witted, or all three? Would you include being good at sports or being artistic? The traditional view of intelligence—and your own intuition—probably would include the first two skills but not the last three. But over the past decade or so, more and more psychologists have argued that there are many different ways to be "intelligent." For example, Peter Salovey argues for two types of intelligence: the traditional cognitive type and a second type that he calls emotional intelligence. Howard Gardner identified even more diverse ways to be intelligent. He identifies a total of seven types of intelligence: bodily, interpersonal, intrapersonal, linguistic, mathematical, musical, and spatial.

In the next reading, Robert Sternberg argues for a triarchic view of intelligence, comprised of analytic ability, creativity, and practical intelligence. In this interview he distinguishes his three-component theory with the two-component and seven-component theories of Salovey and Gardner. Sternberg argues that limiting the definition of intelligence to analytic ability alone results in many smart people being labeled unintelligent. Interestingly, he finds that groups who traditionally fare poorly on I.Q. tests (e.g., lower socioeconomic class and nonwhites) compare much more favorably on his more inclusive three-component I.Q. test.

Melinda Tuhus*
February 18, 1996

Robert J. Sternberg, 46, who is IBM Professor of Psychology and Education Psychology at Yale University, got his undergraduate degree at Yale, his Ph.D. at Stanford, then returned to Yale, where he has been ever since.

In 1988 he published "The Triarchic Mind," which discusses three kinds of intelligence: analytical, practical and creative. (His latest book, "Successful Intelligence," is due out this year.)

Recently, he has challenged the conclusions in "The Bell Curve," Richard Herrnstein and Charles Murray's 1994 book about race and intelligence. Nor is he an admirer of standard methods of intelligence testing—the Scholastic Aptitude Test developed by the Educational Testing Service, for example.

Dr. Sternberg discussed his views in a recent interview in his office at Yale. Following are excerpts from that conversation.

Q. What is intelligence?

A. I call it mental self-management, the manner in which we order and make sense of the events around us or within us.

Q. How did you get interested in this field?

A. I had a negative experience as an undergraduate; I wanted to major in psychology, but I got a C in the intro course. I wasn't good at memorizing, and that's what the course required. So I switched to math. And fortunately, I did even worse. So I switched back to psychology, and, in the upper level courses and in my whole career since, I've never had to memorize anything.

It got me thinking: the system means that you miss a lot of good kids, conversely we get people who are not necessarily the right ones.

Q. What is the triarchic theory?

A. According to the theory, there are three principal aspects of intelligence: analytical—the ability to analyze, judge, evaluate, compare and contrast; creative—the ability to create, design, invent, originate, imagine; and practical—the ability to use, apply, implement, put into practice. Although each can be looked at individually, they are best understood in interaction, since most tasks require a combination of skills.

Q. Does your theory complement or contradict Howard Gardner's theory of seven intelligences?

A. His theory specifies domains of talent: linguistic, logical/mathematical, spatial, musical, bodily/kinesthetic, interpersonal and intrapersonal. It suggests fields of human endeavor. In contrast, the triarchic theory specifies uses of human knowledge for analytical, creative or practical purposes. The two theories are compatible, and in fact, we collaborated to create a program called Practical Intelligence for Schools.

Q. What did you learn?

A. That analytical, creative and practical intelligences can all be developed. People who are successful are those who figure out their strengths and then find ways of capitalizing on them. In the areas they are not good at, they learn enough to get by. The critical thing is to figure out what you have to offer and then make the most of it. But that's not how schools teach at all.

Q. You are said to advocate "intelligent use of intelligence tests." What do you mean by that?

A. We need to expand the kinds of abilities we measure. The kind of test I use measures analytical ability but also creative and practical abilities.

We have both multiple choice and essay and we find that people who do well on one often are not the same people who do well on the other. We also have verbal, quantitative and figural—geometric with no words or numbers—to measure each of the kinds of intelligence.

Q. What did your tests reveal?

A. People who are high creative and high practical were a much more diverse group. The high analytical were mostly white and high income or middle class. The former group had not been seen by their schools as particularly smart. The system is set up to benefit one kind of person, but when you get out in the world it's the creative and practical skills that matter a whole lot more.

Q. Have you put this finding into practice in your research work?

A. We ran a summer program at Yale and recruited high school students nominated by their schools in each of the three areas of intelligence, as well as "high balanced" and "low balanced," meaning they were high or low in all three areas. They all took an advanced placement course in psychology at Yale. But there were different classes based on the different kinds of intelligence. What we found, not surprisingly, is that if you're put in a course that matches your ability, you do better. The only group that preferred the memory course was the "low balanced" group.

Q. For a country that has a history of valuing practical skills, how did we get to this point of focusing on and rewarding just one kind of intelligence, which is not very practical?

A. The system perpetuates itself. For example, people who work at E.T.S. are high-SAT types. People who do well in the system stay, and those who don't do well leave or are kicked out.

Q. You worked at E.T.S. in the summer of 1970. How have tests changed since then?

A. The testing industry is a dinosaur. The first Wechsler adult intelligence scale test came out in 1939, before the Univac computer. In the computer industry if you don't innovate quickly you are dead. But if you don't have competition you don't have to innovate, and that's what's happened with the testing industry.

Q. Another of your areas of research is gifted individuals. What is the problem there?

A. Gifted education is always the first thing to be cut, because people say these kids can get by without special programs. Why we blow off our gifted kids I don't understand.

The biggest problem we have as a society is that today we have to be super-competitive. In global educational competition we don't do well. Our economy is a mess, our political system's a mess. If we don't get with the program we are not going to be competitive.

Q. Do you see a connection between your work and the recently popular notion of "emotional I.Q."?

A. The regulation of emotions is part of translating intelligence into success. Practical and creative intelligence are very important in both interpersonal and international relations.

Q. You're a prolific author. Do you attribute that mainly to analytical intelligence, or do the creative and practical play a significant role?

A. It's an interplay. First you need to have ideas—that's the creative part. Then you have to know which are good ideas—that's analytical. The practical is knowing how to reach a given audience and to write something people will want to read.

Q. About Herrnstein and Murray's "Bell Curve," how would you summarize your critique of their book?

A. There is nothing new in their book. Their book is intellectually dishonest. One thing they do is equate correlation with causation, even though they say they don't do that.

One example of that is when they point out that African Americans consistently score 15 points lower on SAT's than whites, and conclude from that that race is a causal variable. They discuss in detail only one of seven studies on the genetic versus environmental origins of the differences. The other six do not support a genetic interpretation, and the one they do discuss is equivocal.

Their own data do not show that the difference in I.Q. scores is genetic: when they controlled for I.Q. differences, they found telling environmental differences in which blacks were much more likely to be in poverty, to have low birth-weight babies.

Q. Your books don't get the kind of media play as "The Bell Curve." Though often negative, the publicity itself gave their theory more credibility. How do you respond to that?

A. There is pressure to be outrageous. My work is not outrageous enough.

Q. So how do you get the word out?

A. Well, I wrote an introductory psychology textbook that came out last January, called "In Search of the Human Mind." It sold over 40,000 copies in its first edition, which I'm told is very good for a book of that type.

And of course I hope this new book, "Successful Intelligence," will get more publicity. It's about what works in real life, not about what you write on tests.

QUESTIONS

1. Which of the three types of intelligence in Sternberg's theory is closest to the traditional view of intelligence?
2. What does Sternberg mean when he advocates "intelligent use of intelligence tests"? Give an example of what he might call an unintelligent use of intelligence tests.
3. What two explanations does Sternberg give for the failure of intelligence tests to evolve over the past years into something closer to his own theory?
4. How does Sternberg view his theory in relation to that of emotional intelligence? How does he view his theory in relation to Gardner's theory of seven types of intelligence?
5. Reconsider the question raised in the previous reading about how scores on some measure of intelligence have increased in the past decades (e.g., I.Q. tests) while others have decreased (e.g., SAT scores). Can this puzzling finding be explained by Sternberg's distinction?

Section III
Developmental Questions

Reading 11

Movement May Offer Early Clue to Autism

Introduction

Autism, although statistically rare (affecting only about 0.05% of the population), is one of the most common of childhood mental disorders. The effects of autism vary from person to person but typically include unusual social behaviors such as being uninterested in other people (most infants are very interested in other people—see reading 5 about areas of the brain that may influence autistic children's unusual antisocial behavior) and repetitive rituals such as rocking back and forth. Additionally, the severity of autism's effects vary widely: Some autistic children eventually learn to take care of themselves and function independently; others always need to rely on a caregiver for some or most of their daily needs. (A minority of experts believe the mental functioning of people with autism is normal or only slightly affected. This position gained popularity briefly following the development of a technique known as Facilitated Communication, which appeared to show that autistic children are mentally normal but unable to communicate their thoughts. Because the validity of this technique has never been demonstrated, most experts on autism do not trust the results it produced.)

Because the effects of autism on some people are so slight as to allow for almost normal functioning, there is reason to hope that something can be done to ameliorate its effects on all sufferers. One obstacle to this work is the difficulty of early diagnosis. Although the condition is believed to exist from birth, it cannot be reliably diagnosed until several years later when the brain is much less malleable. The following reading, however, offers perhaps the first real hope in early diagnosis. Dr. Philip Teitelbaum believes that autistic infants show particular types of awkwardness when learning to sit up and crawl. Thus it may be possible to identify a child as autistic as early as 6 months, when there may be more time to do something to help.

SANDRA BLAKESLEE*
JANUARY 26, 1999

The discovery that autistic children appear to have subtle abnormalities in body movements that can be diagnosed as early as 3 months is leading researchers to hope for new treatments.

The findings, by Dr. Philip Teitelbaum, a psychologist at the University of Florida in Gainesville, are preliminary. But they have generated intense interest because for the first time, a method is being proposed for diagnosing the condition in babies whose brains are still developing rapidly.

Most autism is not diagnosed in children until they are at least 3 years old. But if there were a reliable way to diagnose autism earlier, Dr. Teitelbaum and other researchers said, doctors might be able to devise therapies to alleviate or eliminate the condition, when the brain is its most malleable.

Autism is a disorder of the brain and behavior that affects about 5 of every 10,000 children. While autistic children appear healthy, they may stare into space for hours, throw tantrums, show no interest in people and pursue repetitive activities, like head banging, with no apparent purpose.

Dr. Teitelbaum made the discovery by examining videotapes of babies who were later found to be autistic. These infants showed a specific cluster of movement abnormalities when rolling over, sitting up, crawling and walking, Dr. Teitelbaum said in a telephone interview.

But, he cautioned, the results are still preliminary. Researchers need to look at many more babies, he said, to see exactly which movement abnormalities can predict autism and which suggest developmental disorders like schizophrenia or attention deficit disorder.

"I think he's on to something," said Dr. Dan Geschwind, a neurogeneticist at the University of California at Los Angeles and scientific adviser to Cure Autism Now, an organization based in Los Angeles run by parents of autistic children. "He's got a very intriguing piece of preliminary data which, if it turns out to be true, will be very important."

Temple Grandin, a highly functioning autistic woman who is an assistant professor of animal science at Colorado State University in Fort Collins and an authority on animal behavior, said: "He's on to something really good and I fully support it. I like the fact that he is objectively measuring something that is biological."

It may be, she cautioned, that Dr. Teitelbaum has discovered general problems in the nervous system that are not unique to autism. But even that, she said, is a benefit for doctors, parents and teachers, who now have nothing to go on before children are 2 or 3 years old.

Dr. Anne Donnellan, a professor of rehabilitation psychology and special education at the University of Wisconsin at Madison, said: "Teitelbaum's work is important because it reflects a reality about autism that has been missed. We tend to think it's a problem with the mind. But now that we are really beginning to see how the brain works, we know that the mind is embodied. Body is part of mind and there's no way to separate them."

Dr. Teitelbaum said that he got the idea of looking at autism as a movement disorder partly because of his work with brain-damaged animals. As they recover, he said, they go through predictable stages, for example recovery of movement, that reflect fundamental aspects of brain organization. Because human babies also pass through predictable stages of development, he theorized that defects in the brain might be reflected in early movements.

A few years ago, Dr. Teitelbaum sent out word to parents of autistic children through various national organizations that he was looking for videotapes of babies before their autism was diagnosed. He received 17 tapes that showed the babies during major milestones of motor development, including rolling over, sitting, crawling, standing and walking.

He also videotaped 15 normal infants as they passed through the same milestones. Portions of each tape were analyzed, using a special technique, for subtle differences in patterns of movement.

No two babies develop motor skills in exactly the same way, but the autistic babies show a specific cluster of movement abnormalities, Dr. Teitelbaum said. Some were subtle and others quite obvious. Normal children may temporarily show some of the same movements.

For example, none of the autistic babies in the tapes learned to roll over like normal children did, he said. Normal babies use a corkscrew motion to go from back to stomach or vice versa. Starting at about 3 months, they first turn their pelvis to one side, followed by the trunk and finally the shoulders and head. By 6 months, the order is reversed: the head goes first and the rest of the body parts follow, corkscrew fashion.

Some of the autistic babies in the tapes never learned to roll over. Others did, but in a peculiar fashion, Dr. Teitelbaum said. Starting from lying on their sides, they rolled to their stomachs or backs by raising heads and pelvises.

Then they threw the upper legs forward and toppled over, moving all body segments together.

And unlike healthy babies who usually learn to sit up at 6 months, even while turning the torso or head, some of the infants whose autism was diagnosed later on toppled easily, failing to one side "like a log" and failing to break the falls with their hands.

Dr. Teitelbaum, who described his findings in a recent issue of the *Proceedings of the National Academy of Sciences,* also noted anomalies in the way the autistic babies in the tapes learned to crawl and walk.

Babies typically start to crawl at about the same time they begin to sit, holding their bodies symmetrically with arms vertical at shoulder width, palms on floor, fingers pointed forward. Thighs are vertical and hip-width apart with knees on the ground and lower legs and feet resting on the floor pointing backward. Weight is commonly distributed equally on all four limbs.

The autistic children in the study showed an asymmetrical lack of support in the arms or legs, Dr. Teitelbaum said. One baby supported himself on his forearms rather than his hands. He raised his pelvis high in the air, bird-dog fashion, but could not move forward. Another baby crawled by scooting his left knee on the floor but used his right foot to push himself forward.

Dr. Teitelbaum said that every autistic child showed some degree of asymmetry in walking. Many tended to shift their weight at the wrong moment, which made their walking appear slightly stiff. Others kept their arms in a more infantile position, arms extended forward. Interestingly, many autistic children walk more slowly and with shorter steps, like Parkinson's disease patients whose motor skills are damaged, Dr. Teitelbaum said.

Early diagnosis has long been a goal of autism researchers, who theorize that the condition results from brain abnormalities that develop before birth. Some researchers think the glitch occurs as early as the 20th to 24th day of gestation, long before women know they are pregnant. Others believe the injury, which could be a mutation or environmental insult, occurs later on, perhaps in the second trimester of pregnancy.

In any event, researchers say that in autistic people, most of the brain forms normally but that some basic scaffolding of nerve fibers is incomplete or improperly developed. Because the human brain grows rapidly in the first year of life—literally constructing circuits that will last a lifetime—this is the best time to intervene.

The goal of intervention would be to stimulate the baby's brain to circumvent the bad wiring or develop connections to compensate for a defect, Dr. Donnellan said. By correcting movements through some form of physical therapy, it may be possible to use feedback to help correct abnormal brain development.

Questions

1. Why is earlier diagnosis of autism potentially important? Developmentally, how does a 3-month-old differ from a 3-year-old?
2. Explain why Grandin worries that the movement style identified in autistic children might not be particular to autistic children but may appear in a broad range of neurological disorders. What additional data would Teitelbaum need to confirm that this style is unique to autism?
3. What movement differences appear to distinguish autistic children? Is there any one type of movement that distinguishes autistic children from developmentally normal children?
4. Why might physical therapy help autistic children's mental functioning?
5. In this exploratory work, Teitelbaum viewed videotapes of children whom he knew to be either autistic or developmentally normal. Should he keep this approach in future investigations? Why or why not?

Reading 12

Two Experts Do Battle Over Potty Training

Introduction

At the turn of the century, John Watson made a bold claim about the effectiveness of parenting methods based on the behaviorist school of psychology he was helping to found. "Give me a dozen healthy infants . . . and I'll guarantee to take any one at random and train him to become any type of specialist I might select—doctor, lawyer, artist, merchant-chief, and yes, even a beggar-man and thief." The way to achieve whatever outcome you wanted for your child was simply to reward desired behaviors and punish undesired behaviors. No doubt you can recall your parents practicing this approach at some point in your own childhood.

But parents today are not as directive as Watson would like. Your parents were likely influenced—either directly or indirectly—by Dr. Benjamin Spock, Dr. T. Berry Brazelton, and other "child-centered" advocates. "Child-centered" parents let their children have more control of childhood decisions instead of deciding everything themselves. One of the most important decisions that children must have a say in, according to Brazelton, is when to begin using the toilet. Letting children wait until they are ready has led to a considerable increase in the average age at which children achieve toilet mastery. It has also led to a considerable increase in average profits for the diaper companies. In the following reading, Brazelton, John Rosemond, and other child experts argue about whether parents should return to a more behaviorist tradition of deciding for their children when to begin using the toilet.

There is one point of agreement between the two schools of thought: Potty training may very well have important psychological consequences for children. Freud was the first psychologist to suggest that toilet training may affect adult personality. He believed some parents were too rigid and others too relaxed during this critical period and that either extreme led to undesired personality characteristics in adulthood. Freud's concerns are echoed in this reading: Rosemond warns that American parents have become too relaxed and Brazelton argues they are still too rigid.

Erica Goode*
January 12, 1999

Toilet training is not rocket science, says John Rosemond, a syndicated columnist and best-selling author of parenting books. He considers it "a slap to the intelligence of a human being that one would allow him to continue soiling and wetting himself past age 2." The process, he says, should be as simple and straightforward as housebreaking a 4-month-old puppy.

The noted pediatrician T. Berry Brazelton says there is more to it than that. Parents who force toilet training, he says, can cause lasting problems. "Don't rush your toddler into toilet training or let anyone else tell you it's time—it's got to be his choice," Dr. Brazelton advises in a television commercial for Pampers size-6 diapers, suitable for children 35 pounds and over.

What does he think about Mr. Rosemond's arguments? "They sound very logical—for a puppy."

So goes the newest round in the toilet-training wars.

The previous round was won by parenting experts like Dr. Brazelton and Dr. Benjamin Spock, who schooled a generation of 1960's parents in a flexible toilet-training approach.

But over the last few decades, the age at which toddlers become diaper-free has been creeping upward. In 1957, 92 percent of children were toilet-trained by the age of 18 months, studies found. Today the figure for 2-year-olds is just 4 percent, according to a large-scale Philadelphia study. Only 60 percent of children have achieved mastery of the toilet by 36 months, the study found, and 2 percent remain untrained at the age of 4 years.

Moreover, though there are no hard statistics on them, pediatricians say they are seeing more children with toilet-training problems, including withholding of urine and stool, chronic constipation, and wetting and soiling by older children. Dr. Bruce Filmer, an associate professor at Thomas Jefferson University Medical School in Philadelphia, for example, says he and other pediatric urologists have noticed an increase in referrals of young patients experiencing problems with both daytime and nighttime urinary control.

These developments combined have fed a multibillion-dollar diaper industry, which last year had training-pant sales of $545 million, and have

*Reprinted with permission from *The New York Times.*

spurred the introduction of the giant-sized diaper, designed for toddlers well past the terrible 2's.

The sight of diaper-clad 3- and 4-year-olds does not amuse Mr. Rosemond, a family psychologist who advocates a return to traditional child-rearing practices, and he has decided to do public battle on the issue.

In a series of columns last month, published in more than 100 newspapers, he attributed delayed training to wishy-washy parenting inspired by "Freudian mumbo jumbo." In particular, he pointed to Dr. Brazelton, professor emeritus of pediatrics at Harvard Medical School, who in the 1960's pioneered the "child-centered" parenting approach, recommending that parents let their children decide when to become diaper-free.

The increasing tendency for parents to leave the timing of toilet training up to the child, Mr. Rosemond asserted, is largely responsible for the rise in toilet-training difficulties. Delayed training, he said in a telephone interview, can also lead to discipline problems, because mothers spend too much time being servants for their children and do not make the transition soon enough to "authority figure."

Mr. Rosemond concedes that Dr. Brazelton has been giving the same advice for decades but also criticizes him for serving as a consultant to Pampers, a product of the Procter & Gamble Company, and for appearing in the Pampers commercial.

"I think it's a fairly blatant conflict of interest," Mr. Rosemond said.

For his part, Dr. Brazelton said he believed that the rise in toilet training problems was a result of too much pressure on children, not too little. The increase can be traced to the escalating demands of modern life, he said. Day-care centers often require that children be toilet-trained in order to enroll, and working parents end up leaning on them to comply. Parents share the responsibility for training with nannies and baby sitters, a circumstance that children may find confusing.

"Parents are feeling very guilty, and people like Rosemond are making them feel more guilty, not less," Dr. Brazelton said. "And the child's only recourse is to withhold urine or stool in protest."

As for his relationship with Pampers, which provides financing for his research and health care projects, Dr. Brazelton said he was proud of the association.

"It took me a long time to decide to do it, but I'm absolutely convinced that it was a wonderful thing to do," he said. "I'm certainly not doing it to keep kids in diapers. It's just the opposite: Pampers is willing to go along with me to make it easier for mothers to let kids be open to toilet training when they are ready."

To "go along," of course, is not all that difficult for Procter & Gamble, which, like its competitor Kimberly-Clark, maker of Huggies, recognizes a bonanza when it sees it.

Wendy Strong, director of corporate communications for Kimberly-Clark, said the company's own marketing research confirmed that toddlers were toilet training later than in the past: only 12 percent of children are trained at 18 months, the company found, and 85 percent by 30 months. Huggies, too, just began offering customers a size-6 diaper, but the company also makes "training pants" for toddlers of 38 pounds or more, a product category, Ms. Strong said, that Kimberly-Clark "expects to grow to more than a billion dollars by 2002."

Whichever expert's school of parenting a toddler's parents decide to follow, they run no risk of confusing the philosophies, or the methods themselves.

Mr. Rosemond offers a toilet-training technique he calls "naked and $75," which he recommends that parents embark upon with their 2-year-olds.

"You stay home from work with your child for a few days," he said, and "you let the child walk around the house naked all day long." The parent puts the potty where the child spends most of his time, and moves it when necessary to keep it nearby. Every so often, the parent reminds the child to use the potty when needed.

"Children at this age do not like urine and feces running down their legs," Mr. Rosemond said. "When they have an accident, they stop and start to howl, and the mother comes along and says, 'Well, you forgot to use the toilet.' She puts him on the toilet, wipes him off, speaks reassuringly to him. And within three days, or five days, he's doing it on his own."

The $75, he added, is for the carpet cleaning.

In contrast, Dr. Brazelton, like Mr. Rosemond the author of best-selling parenting manuals, discourages parents from expecting their child to potty-train in a few days. He recommends that parents buy a potty chair and "show children what is expected of them at 2, what we are all doing and why it is important."

But, he says, the rate at which training occurs should be left up to the child.

"If your child is afraid of the potty chair, don't put pressure on him to use it," Dr. Brazelton advises in a step-by-step guide available on the Pampers Parenting Institute's Web site (www.pampers.com). "Put toilet training aside for a month or two, and give your child time to get used to the idea of the potty and to be comfortable with it."

"Be patient and positive," the pediatrician suggests. "As with any new skill, your child will master toilet training in time."

In his experience, Dr. Brazelton said, 85 percent to 90 percent of children will embrace toilet training soon after they first show an interest.

"But the others are saying that there are other issues they're trying to deal with," he said, "like day care, like parents who are extremely busy. The child gets confused and maybe even angry, and withholds. And at this point I think you have to be able to say, 'This has got to be up to you.'"

For parents, the bottom line seems to be: Whatever works.

Melissa Saren, for example, a Manhattan lawyer, said she tried introducing her son Matthew to the potty when he was 3. "But I think looking back on it that I started when I was ready, not when he was ready," she said.

For months, nothing seemed to work, not bribes, not the books "Once Upon a Potty" or "Everyone Poops," not "big boy" underwear. Finally, she said, Matthew decided the time was right—when he enrolled in day care at 3½.

"Seeing the other boys poop in the potty" seemed to do the trick, Ms. Saren said. "I would fall into the category of thinking that you just leave them alone and they'll come to it."

Other mothers—Mr. Rosemond said his daughter-in-law was one example—find that the "stay at home and do it in three days" approach works just fine.

But many pediatricians say their experience has landed them much closer to the Brazelton camp than the Rosemond. Dr. Filmer, for example, said he had seen many parents become embroiled in battles with their children if they try to force toilet training within a defined period of time.

"Goodness me," Dr. Filmer said, "you talk to these parents and they will tell you that their children formed almost a fear of toilet training."

Dr. Bruce Taubman, a pediatrician in the department of gastroenterology and nutrition at Children's Hospital in Philadelphia who has a private practice in Cherry Hill, N.J., said: "To get a child trained by 2 can be done, but it is probably done at a cost. It takes a tremendous effort."

But Dr. Taubman said he had a hunch, though he did not yet have data to support it, that there was a window of opportunity, perhaps near the age of 2 or 2½, "when kids really want their parents to get excited if the kids poop." If this opportunity is missed, toilet training may take much longer.

Dr. Taubman is one of the few people who have collected systematic data on toilet training. In 1997, he published the first large-scale study of children's reactions to toilet training since the 1960's, a report on 482 children in suburban Philadelphia. The study appeared in the journal *Pediatrics*.

In addition to assessing the ages at which most children now train, Dr. Taubman found that boys trained later than girls on average and that the average age at which parents introduced toilet training was 23 months.

There is no relationship, Dr. Taubman found, between when a child is trained and the mother's work status, the presence of siblings, the child's scores on measures of behavior, or whether the child is in day care.

About 13 percent of the children in the study had trouble with toilet training, withholding stool or refusing to use the toilet. But the vast majority of these children, Dr. Taubman said, "resolved the problem without intervention."

Questions

1. What percentage of 18-month-olds were toilet trained in 1957? What percentage of 18-month-olds are toilet trained today? Using the statistics in this reading, estimate for how many more months parents must buy diapers for their children today.
2. How, according to Rosemond, can delayed toilet training affect discipline problems? What evidence does he cite to support this claim?
3. Brazelton argues that increased toilet training problems are the result of too much pressure placed on children, not too little. How does he reconcile this argument with the age trend discussed in question 1?
4. What factors did Taubman find to predict age of toilet training? What factors did not predict toilet training? Can you offer explanations of these findings?
5. Describe briefly the relationship between Brazelton and Pampers. Do any aspects of this relationship make you question Brazelton's objectivity?

Reading 13

The Hype and Hope of Reading to Baby

Introduction

Most parents obviously want their children to grow up healthy and happy. But more than that, the great majority hope their children will do well in school and be successful in life. But for centuries the conventional wisdom of parenting was different. Just a century ago, most people believed intelligence was determined primarily by such factors as one's race, family status, and skull size. Parents thus had little reason to worry about the intellectual environment in which their children grew up. But over the past decades, psychologists began to believe that intellectual development is affected by early experience in the home. The current conventional wisdom for parents is, accordingly, they should do all they can to stimulate children's natural intellectual abilities from a very young age.

In this next reading, this current conventional wisdom is challenged. Specifically, the idea that reading to children at a very early age (birth to 3 years) can increase their verbal ability or general school performance is challenged. The attack comes from a controversial new book, The Nurture Assumption, *by Judith Harris. Harris argues that nothing parents do can affect their children a great deal. Among the efforts that parents make but that are wasted on them, she includes reading to children. Not surprisingly, her argument that parents do not matter has created a stir of controversy. In this next reading, specialists from a variety of perspectives argue over how to interpret the small amount of data that speak to the question of whether reading to children matters.*

Doreen Carvajal*
September 6, 1998

For baby's literary enlightenment, the hand that rocks the cradle should also be turning the pages of "Good Night Moon" or "The Poky Little Puppy."

At least that's the hope of an assortment of major publishers seeking to raise a new generation of book buyers. It's also the goal of a growing number of charities and foundations that have brought together pediatricians, volunteers and librarians in a less commercial quest to promote the notion that reading aloud to toddlers, babies—even newborns—is a child-care ritual as vital as mother's milk.

The problem is that there's little evidence that reading aloud to infants and toddlers has any dramatic benefit. "The general consensus is that it's important, but it may be of relatively modest provable effect based on current research," acknowledged Robert Needleman, a Cleveland pediatrician and a research consultant for Reach Out and Read, a national program that encourages pediatricians to "prescribe" story reading for children at their checkups. Dr. Needleman added, however, that "What has been shown is that you can make small but significant differences in their verbal ability."

But the lack of definitive baby-literacy research has not slowed profit-oriented publishers and literacy advocates—even as their logic has come under attack from a provocative new book on developmental psychology that has generated hyperbolic magazine headlines about whether parents' efforts to mold their children really matter very much.

The book, "The Nurture Assumption: Why Children Turn Out the Way They Do" (Free Press), by Judith Rich Harris, maintains that parents aren't as important as children's peers and society at large in determining adult behavior.

Peer Pressure

"The evidence suggesting that reading to children makes them smarter in school is ambiguous evidence," Mrs. Harris said. "The fact that there is a correlation between reading to a child and a child doing well in school can be due to different reasons. Perhaps it does have an effect. But other evidence suggests that's not the case. That could be due to the genetic effects of parents who like to read."

Mrs. Harris questions the view that parents can affect a child's personality and temperament. "The nurture assumption is a 20th-century belief that has turned into a myth in a very exaggerated form," she said. "It has almost become a religion that parents have to do this and that. And if they don't, their children will be irrevocably damaged. This has placed a very heavy burden on parents. They're feeling guilty and intimidated that one misstep will ruin their child for life."

Not surprisingly, Mrs. Harris's views about the limits of parental influence are heresy to reading advocates, though she said she generally supported reading aloud to babies—sticking to her theory that if the broader society and peer groups value reading, then so eventually will children.

To support the merits of baby literacy, groups like the Association of American Publishers and the American Academy of Pediatricians cite the positive impact of reading aloud on brain development. A fact sheet issued by the publishers' association summarizing recent research asserts: "A child-care provider reads to a toddler. And in a matter of seconds, thousands of cells in these children's growing brains respond. Some brain cells are 'turned on,' triggered by this particular experience."

But the scientific evidence is less clear. Richard N. Aslin, a professor in the brain and cognitive sciences department at the University of Rochester, has been studying infants from birth to 12 months old to determine how well they hear speech. By repeating nonsense words to babies and watching their movements, Mr. Aslin said, his research has shown that babies are quicker learners than usually given credit for.

"The brain does develop rapidly very early in life, but it's not clear whether these kinds of brain development are so critical that you have to have certain kinds of experiences to develop normally," Professor Aslin said. "We just don't know."

Nonetheless, efforts to promote baby literacy continue to gather steam. The William Penn Foundation recently spent more than $2.5 million on a program promoting reading in 300 Philadelphia day-care centers with more than 18,000 children, many of them under the age of 3.

The publishers' association and the Boston-based Institute for Civil Society are planning to imitate this program in other cities in a campaign tentatively called "Books for Babies." In addition, Scholastic, a leading publisher of children's books, is sponsoring a tour by the author Rosemary Wells to promote "Read to Your Bunny," a picture book about the rewards of reading 20 minutes a day to young children. And HarperCollins has been expanding its line of books labeled for age groups from newborn to 3-year-olds.

Broad Efforts

Patricia Schroeder, the former Colorado Representative and chief executive of the publisher's association, has also jumped on the baby-buggy campaign. For her son's wedding in July, 750 copies of "Read to Your Bunny" were donated to Easton Hospital in Pennsylvania in lieu of traditional gifts to the bridesmaids and ushers.

These broader efforts might actually have their desired effect, Mrs. Harris contends—regardless of a parent's specific storytelling rituals. "If a child grows up in a culture where most of the parents do read to children and books are important, then that child is going to pick up that culture, first at home and then when they go out," she said.

Questions

1. According to Needleman, does reading to children improve their verbal ability?
2. Why, according to Harris, is the evidence connecting reading with better school performance equivocal? What alternative hypothesis does she suggest may account for it? Can you suggest a different alternative explanation?
3. Given her belief that reading to children cannot affect them, why does she say she still does it? Is this consistent with her genetic interpretation of reading ability?
4. What evidence does the Association of American Publishers cite to support their claim of the importance of reading? Does this evidence seem compelling to you?
5. Consider Harris's two arguments from questions 2 and 3. How would each position view the William Penn Foundation's program to promote reading in Philadelphia day-care centers?

Reading 14

After Girls Get the Attention, Focus Shifts to Boy's Woes

Introduction

As we saw in the previous reading, parents wanting to do the best for their children often hear conflicting advice about parenting strategies. Whereas the previous reading focused on strategies that may (or may not) help children reach their full intellectual potential, Carey Goldberg's article focuses on strategies to help children develop in socially and emotionally healthy ways. The reading begins by citing evidence that American boys are not, as a whole, doing particularly well. Compared to girls, boys are twice as likely to die during the teenage years, twice as likely to be learning disabled, four times as likely to be emotionally disturbed, and six times as likely to be diagnosed with an attention-deficit disorder.

Such statistics as these suggest that the way we treat young boys is working less well than the way we treat young girls. Unfortunately, there is a great deal of disagreement over exactly what differences in our treatment of boys and girls are to blame. To make matters worse, there is very little empirical data to draw on to help us evaluate the different claims about how to solve the problem. In this reading you will hear some blame boys' woes on the traditional parenting style that is too accepting and encouraging of aggressiveness in boys. Yet others blame parents and schools that are not accepting enough of aggressiveness in boys; it is our failure to accommodate boys' natural roughness that causes their emotional distress and learning disabilities. Who is right? As you read the article, consider carefully the kinds of evidence each child-rearing expert provides as well as the kinds of evidence they do not provide.

Carey Goldberg*
April 23, 1998

Every April for six years now, as millions of girls have tagged along on Take Our Daughters to Work Day, there has been a pained counterpoint to the training under way, a parenthetical murmur. ("But what about our sons?")

A similar objection met reports on how schools short-change girls. ("But don't our boys seem at least as distressed?") And research on how girls' self-esteem crashes at puberty. ("But boys die a thousand deaths, too!")

Now, increasingly, such parenthetical protests are translating into a surge of head-on exploration—from academic research to workshops and parents' groups to a rash of books coming out in the next few months—all meant to address what some people call a cultural threat to American boys that is different, but no less serious, from the one facing girls.

"Four boys are diagnosed as emotionally disturbed to every one girl," said Michael Gurian, a psychotherapist in Spokane, Wash., and author of the top-selling "The Wonder of Boys" (Tarcher/Putnam, 1996). "In education, two boys are learning disabled for every one girl."

"In grades, our boys now get worse grades than our girls. If we go to brain-attention disorders, there are six boys with attention-deficit disorder to every one girl. If we go to teen deaths, there are two teen boys dying for every one girl. Should I keep going? I can rattle off 50 of these."

Drawing much of its intellectual grounding from research and writing being done around Boston, the incipient boys' movement focuses on the deepening difficulties of being a boy in the current American culture. With the vanguard ranging from prominent academics like Carol Gilligan, the Harvard psychologist, to coffee groups of confused and seeking parents, it calls attention to the dangers of seeing what used to be considered natural boyish behavior as something pathological.

At the same time, the movement casts light on how age-old ways of rearing boys to conform to the norms of "Real Man-hood" can brutalize and scar them emotionally. From the shootings in Jonesboro, Ark., to the millions of boys on the drug Ritalin, the new boys' advocates say, signs abound that boys are in emotional distress.

For all the dark statistics, the boys' movement focuses on the positive side of boyhood as well. Using current neuroscience and common sense, it seeks to help parents and teachers understand what makes boys tick rather than demonize them as aggressive, and to rear boys to be sweet and feeling as well as tough.

Though the boys' movement might seem to be pulling some of the blanket away from girls, its potential to improve relations between the sexes

---

has won the support of the likes of Marie C. Wilson, president of the Ms. Foundation for Women, which created the annual Take Our Daughters to Work Day, observed on Thursday.

"I feel like our attention to girls actually engendered this new attention to boys," Ms. Wilson said. "It used to be when we talked about gender, we just meant women. This is such a relief!"

Still, some boys' advocates blame feminism for leaving a streak of anti-male sentiment in American culture that creates problems for boys.

Barb Wilder-Smith, a teacher and researcher who has run several "mothers-of-sons" discussion groups in the Boston area and just completed a book on boys' fantasy play, says she has found that "we believe badness is in boys."

It has reached the point, Ms. Wilder-Smith said, that when she made T-shirts reading, "Boys Are Good," they raised objections among the student teachers she trains (one of whom was wearing a button reading, "So Many Men, So Little Intelligence"). And when her young son wore a T-shirt extolling boys, she said, a woman driver stopped her car to say, "Boys are good? Well, girls are better."

Problem That Appears At Start of School

In the struggle to understand what goes wrong for boys, researchers are turning more and more to the early years and a crisis that seems to hit many boys around the time they enter school. Dr. Gilligan, the Harvard psychologist who did pioneering work on girls over the last two decades, has begun observing 4-year-old boys in pursuit of a hypothesis that others share.

Dr. Gilligan's hunch, said Judy Chu, a doctoral candidate working with her, "is that just as adolescent girls struggle with their socialization towards cultural constructions of femininity, boys may experience a similar struggle in early childhood, which is when they are faced with heightened pressures to conform more rigidly to cultural constructions of masculinity. Studies have shown there are parallel symptoms of psychological distress among boys—depression and evidence of struggle and conflict."

What happens at that age?

First, "they're thrown into schools where, on average, boys aren't as good at things as girls," said Michael Thompson, a Boston-area psychologist who is co-writing a book, "Raising Cain: Protecting the Emotional Life of Boys." "Girls read faster and sit more nicely and boys are more physically restless and impulsive.

"And we sometimes don't make accommodations for the boys' developmental levels, so we humiliate them and get them mad, or interpret their activity as willful aggression, and so begins the fulfillment of a prophecy where we try to punish and control boys more harshly than girls, and they come to resent it and dislike it and dislike authority and react back against it."

At around the same time, said Dr. William Pollack, a Harvard psychiatrist whose years of studying boys led him to write "Real Boys: Rescuing Our Sons from the Myths of Boyhood," to be published soon by Random House, boys are undergoing another difficult process, striking out on their own when they would still like to be clinging to mothers' legs.

"We prematurely separate boys from their mothers and nurturing in general in a way we don't do to girls," Dr. Pollack said. "And we call that normal boy development, and my argument is that not only isn't it normal but it's traumatic, and that trauma has major consequences."

What results, some psychologists and teachers say, is boys who become emotionally cut off and less able to experience empathy and absorb moral teachings.

"Boys were traditionally raised to be soldiers and every toy and cartoon dealt with not having feelings, and you could hurt people and nothing would happen," said Merry-Murray Meade, a kindergarten teacher at the Atrium School, a private elementary school in Watertown, Mass. Now, Ms. Meade said: "We want little boys to take on feelings. But the fathers often don't even know how to do it. They say, 'If I bring that out in him, will he be a girl?'"

In adolescence, said Dan Kindlon, a Harvard Medical School psychology professor co-writing "Raising Cain," boys are further isolated and stunted by what he calls a "culture of cruelty."

"In the period of seventh, eighth and ninth grade, boys learn that to show vulnerability is akin to death," Dr. Kindlon said. "You talk to a 75-year-old man and he can still remember the names he was called then."

Black and Hispanic boys can experience particular problems in adolescence, researchers say, because when they act peer-pleasingly tough, adults see them as dangerous and threatening, but if they act soft, they are likelier to be victimized. The suicide rate for black adolescent boys, though still proportionally lower than that of white boys, has gone up 100 percent over the last 10 years, Dr. Pollack said.

Put the psychological picture together, stir in recent biological findings on everything from the effects of testosterone to sex differences in brains, and an array of scary statistics begin to make sense, boys' advocates argue.

In his forthcoming book about adolescents, "A Fine Young Man" (Tarcher/Putnam), Mr. Gurian notes that adolescent boys are four times more likely than girls to commit suicide (though girls try more often) and the number of boys' suicides are rising while the number for girls are not. Four times as many adolescent boys drop out of high school as girls, including girls who have babies.

Many Are Diagnosed With Attention Deficit

Of particular concern to many is the epidemic levels at which young American boys are being diagnosed with attention-deficit disorder and prescribed Ritalin. A lunchtime line of pill-takers has become a common scene at many school nurses' offices, and many boys' advocates say that Ritalin is greatly over-prescribed.

"I'd say what those boys really have is not attention-deficit disorder but M.D.D.—male-deficit disorder," Dr. Pollack said. "We see boys as deficient because we have models of development that are not empathic to boys."

Relying on recent neuroscientific research, Mr. Gurian and others argue that boys' behavior is often biologically based. Boys' high energy and love of games that involve pursuit and moving objects results from eons of evolution as hunters, for example. Society, the boys' advocates say, is trying to quash history.

Commercially speaking, the bushel of books on boys coming out may be merely an effort by publishers to recapture the success of Mary Pipher's "Reviving Ophelia," which only recently fell off *The Times* best-seller list after 148 weeks. But the authors of the boys' books and other researchers see themselves as part of a chorus calling for change in how boys are reared, and offer concrete remedies from different ways of playing to different ways of listening.

Many of their suggestions are geared to mothers who have been so baffled by sons who, given dolls, rip off their heads and use their bodies as guns, or who find a sudden painful distance between themselves and their boys.

"Women have to learn to speak boys' language as well as boys speaking women's," said Barney Brawer, a former school principal now at Tufts University who, with Dr. Gilligan, co-directed a two-year Harvard Project on Women's Psychology, Boys' Development and the Culture of Manhood. That often means bonding with their sons as fathers have, "side by side," during a shared activity, rather than face to face, he said, or more subtle communication than "What's wrong?"

Ms. Wilder-Smith said she also tried to help mothers and teachers accept and interpret the rowdiness often inherent in boys' play rather than trying to squelch it.

"Most classrooms have rules against play that involves guns or shooting or bad guys," she said. "It's a backlash against the violence in our culture, but I'm afraid we've made boys pathological—what we used to see as normal. We're rejecting the culture of masculinity and trying to redefine it, but we're throwing out the boy with the bathwater."

Offering Alternatives In Rearing of Boys

Many of the boys' advocates also push for boys spending more time in all-boy environments, whether in single-sex schools and classes or in activities like Scouting.

In the Seattle area, for example, Peter Wallis, a longtime teacher and camp director, puts together boys' seminars and weekends that incorporate ideas from Mr. Gurian's book in a mix of physical exercise and myth. He has the boys act out dramatic stories and "hero quests" that emphasize "the classical vision of males as noble beings with diverse abilities," Mr. Wallis said.

And educators talk about gearing school activities to be more boy-friendly, for example allowing more learning-by-doing, such as a recent project at the Atrium School that allowed children to try chipping at rocks in the schoolyard as they studied the Stone Age and to build their own primitive inventions.

Others push for different forms of interaction with girls. At the Atrium School, Samuel Shem, a psychiatrist, and his wife, Janet Surrey, a psychologist, are experimenting with boy-girl "gender dialogues" to help them understand each other.

Dr. Shem worries that the boys' movement will become too much like "Robert Bly for boys," he said, referring to the drum-beating, woods-going men's movement.

"If you buy into the let-men-be-men view, you end up with a lot of lonely men in middle age," he said. "What I'm saying is all human beings have the same nature, which is to want to be in a good connection, and all you're doing with boys is to come back to what they experience early in life, and give them what they yearn for."

Some girls' advocates also maintain that the boys' movement is merely more patriarchal business as usual, grabbing attention away from girls' problems just when they have gained a brief spotlight after millennia of neglect and oppression.

But those like Ms. Wilson hold out hope that ultimately, girls could benefit as well from a boys' movement.

"We'd be so naive to think we could change the lives of girls without boys' lives changing," she said.

Questions

1. What specific problem was the Take Our Daughters to Work Day designed to address? Do young girls still have a greater need than young boys for such a program?

2. According to Thompson, what happens to boys at school that may result in their later distrust of authority? What evidence would convince you of Thompson's theory? Does he provide such evidence?
3. Why does Pollak feel the situation is worse for black and Hispanic boys than for white boys?
4. How does Wilder-Smith view the typical male behavior of rowdiness? How does this differ from the view taken by that attributed to Gilligan (near the beginning of the article)? What approach would each suggest for solving boys' emotional distress?
5. Do you believe paying attention to boys' emotional problems will take attention away from girls' emotional problems? Do you think that programs which focus on girls' issues—such as Take Our Daughters to Work Day—negatively affect boys?

Reading 15

Exploring Physical Beauty as a Psychological Weapon

Introduction

You might wonder why a reading on physical beauty appears in a book of readings for psychology. Can beauty affect our psychological development? The unfortunate truth is that it can and does. Beauty is an important topic in social psychology because most people hold stereotypes about attractiveness. Attractive people are believed to be nicer, more socially skilled, and more worth knowing. Conversely, unattractive people are believed to have a number of unfavorable traits. If you watch your own behavior you will probably notice that you are more eager to talk to or make friends with people who are physically attractive.

Beauty is also an important topic in developmental psychology because it affects our social development. Because children's peers and even their teachers treat them differently if they are attractive or unattractive, physical appearance affects our development of self-esteem. In childhood, attractive children seem only to benefit from the extra attention given them by friends and teachers. But later in life attractive adults may become depressed as their looks fade with age or if they come to suspect that people are nice to them because of their attractiveness and not for their inner personality.

In addition to the psychological consequences of beauty, psychologists also worry about the threat to physical health that comes when women or men starve themselves to obtain an unrealistic beauty ideal. For all of these reasons, beauty is a concern for psychologists. In this next reading, a panel of various experts considers our obsession with beauty and what should be done about it.

KATE STONE LOMBARDI*
OCTOBER 26, 1997

"Forget homilies like 'Beauty is as beauty does,' " Nancy Friday, the author of several pop psychology books, said. "Believe me, beauty is a player, stalking the streets bare-breasted, stiletto heeled, fly unzipped. Its power is luminous and monumental."

Clearly, Ms. Friday was not discussing inner beauty. In a freewheeling address to a women's conference at the Westchester Division of the New York Hospital-Cornell Medical Center here, Ms. Friday, best known for her book "My Mother/Myself" (Delacorte) and most recently the author of "The Power of Beauty" (HarperCollins), variously discussed her childhood ("Believe me, I was not a pretty adolescent,") the night she met her current husband ("a night of truly spectacular sex,") and her relationship with her mother ("Our mothers' eyes are our first mirror. In order to survive, I had to tell myself that with her gaze my mother saw me and loved me.")

The disconnected impressions, the extrapolation of personal experience into cultural theory and the breathless, stream-of-consciousness delivery that marked Ms. Friday's talk was not the usual fare for the 100-year-old psychiatric hospital, which is known for its comprehensive treatment of various mental illnesses and conditions.

The Women's Conference is part of the hospital's community-education program, which is meant to reach beyond the population it has traditionally served.

Ms. Friday's talk was followed by a panel discussion, "Beneath the Surface," which explored the psychology of beauty and society's obsession with physical attractiveness. The panel, which featured professionals in social work, as well as a specialist in eating disorders and a sex therapist, addressed the subject in somewhat more clinical terms.

The panelists agreed that physical beauty is a powerful phenomenon. Research has revealed that being attractive conveys pronounced social and psychological advantages throughout life. Pretty children get more attention from teachers than plain ones, while more attractive adults earn more money than their less appealing peers.

Studies have also shown that other people tend to associate beautiful women and handsome men with goodness. Research done by Diane Hatfield, a psychologist at the University of Hawaii, and the author of "Mirror, Mirror . . ." (State University of New York Press) revealed that people tend to assume that attractive people are warm, sensitive, kind, interesting, poised and outgoing.

Good looks are also big business, said a panelist, Linda Quinn, the service line coordinator for the Outpatient Eating Disorders Clinic at the hospital. "Billions of dollars are invested annually to keep us dissatisfied with how we

---

look," Ms. Quinn said. About $20 billion a year is spent on the cosmetics industry and another $33 billion on the diet industry, according to figures from "The Beauty Myth" (William Morrow) by Naomi Wolf.

The quest for beauty is also a major driving force behind the rising popularity of cosmetic surgery, a $300 million a year industry. A survey by the American Society of Plastic and Reconstructive Surgeons revealed that those who approve of surgery, both for themselves and for others, for esthetic reasons has risen 50 percent in the last decade.

While women still make up the vast majority of cosmetic surgery patients—liposuction and breast implants remain the two most popular procedures—men, too, have face lifts, fat siphoned off and even silicone implants inserted into chests and calves to create a more muscular look. Hair-replacement treatments to combat baldness are also on the rise.

Politicians are well versed in the importance of looks to their success. Pundits have long held that it was Richard M. Nixon's 5 o'clock shadow that caused him to lose the first televised debate with John F. Kennedy in 1960. Radio listeners attributed victory to Mr. Nixon, but television viewers believed the more clean-shaven and decidedly less sweaty Mr. Kennedy was the winner. Candidates have paid attention ever since. In the last Presidential election, advisers told Bob Dole to smile more; they advised President Clinton to lose weight.

While Ms. Friday in her talk suggested that women did themselves a disservice in pretending that looks do not matter and urged them to use beauty's power, the panel members expressed concern about society's fixation on good looks. Mary Hanrahan, the director of program development and planning of the outpatient department of the Payne Whitney Clinic at New York Hospital-Cornell Medical Center, recalled a patient who walked into her office who was so physically stunning that the therapist was momentarily in awe.

"She was a top-flight New York model, absolutely gorgeous, but within one session what was profoundly coming across was that she had beauty but she thought she had little else," Ms. Hanrahan said. "Her sense of herself was that she was all face and figure. We went on a journey to see what else was there."

The flip side of the equation—those who think they will never match up to society's concept of beauty and feel empty because of it—was the concern of Ms. Quinn, whose professional practice focuses on trying to save the lives of young women who are starving themselves to the point of death. She said that since the 1960's, beauty has been defined as being thin, and that the ideal body weight today is 20 percent thinner than it was three decades ago. Only 1 percent of women can achieve this body type without what she called "heroic measures."

Ms. Quinn added that while the causes of eating disorders are complex, it is still in the "dichotomy between the ideal and real where eating disorders have flourished." She referred to a Glamour magazine survey of 33,000 women, in which 75 percent of women considered themselves fat, while insurance tables found only 25 percent of them fat. She said that women with eating disorders did not think very differently from unafflicted women, but that their activities went to extremes.

A panelist, Dr. Miriam Baker, a sex therapist with the Helen Kaplan Institute, said that the biggest obstacle to women's sexual pleasure was their negative thoughts about their bodies. "Anti-fantasies about our body dramatically interfere with the basic ability to achieve sexual fulfillment, because our sexual pleasure derives from the way we feel about how we look," she said.

Ms. Friday expressed impatience with those she referred to as "anti-men, anti-sex matriarchal feminists." She blamed her mother for teaching her that her sexual organs were "dirty and disgusting." She recalled her adolescence in South Carolina, where she learned to stand with bent knees under her skirts, so that she would not appear taller than boys, which was followed by a triumphant arrival in New York City, where she discovered she was actually attractive to men.

Still, her book about beauty reveals a poignant ambiguity that her talk did not.

She writes: "Twenty years later, I would go through countless hours of physical therapy to realign my spine, which has never recovered from the bent-leg posture I mastered in learning the art of being less. Neither professional success, great friendships nor the love of men could recapture the self-confidence, the inner vision and, yes, the kindness and generosity I owned before I lost myself in the external mirrors of adolescence."

QUESTIONS

1. How are attractive and unattractive children treated? How do attractive and unattractive adults fare on the job market? Might the two be related?
2. In *Glamour* magazine's survey of 33,000 women, what percentage of women consider themselves to be fat despite being within their ideal weight range? Do you think this figure is representative of all American women? Discuss the methodology of this survey in forming your answer.
3. How have attitudes toward plastic surgery changed over the past few years? In light of her comments in this reading, do you think Friday would approve of this trend?
4. Why might Quinn argue with Friday's opinion of how to deal with our society's obsession with attractiveness in its current form?
5. Why does the author of this reading point to Friday's discussion of her physical therapy to realign her spine as a "poignant ambiguity"? What message does this story tell that seems absent from Friday's talk?

Section IV
Personality and Social Behavior

Reading 16

Self-Image Is Suffering from Lack of Esteem

Introduction

Are you more likely to agree with the statement "on the whole, I am satisfied with myself" or that "at times I think I am no good at all"? These two items appear on one of the most often used measures of self-esteem: the Rosenberg self-esteem scale. As you must have guessed, people who endorse the first item more than the second are said to have higher self-esteem.

Most people believe that self-esteem and intelligence are the two most important personality variables. Low levels of either intelligence or self-esteem are probably the two most common explanations for why some people fail where others succeed. Earlier, in readings 9 and 10, we read that although psychologists do not all agree about what intelligence is, most still believe it to be important for success. In the next reading we see that not only do psychologists disagree about what self-esteem is, but new research calls into question the idea that it is necessary or sufficient to be successful. Among the puzzling findings under the old assumptions of self-esteem is that prison inmates have about the same level of self-esteem as college students. Findings such as this one require a completely new conceptualization of self-esteem.

KIRK JOHNSON*
MAY 5, 1998

Self-esteem had it all, once.

Common sense and research had shown that people who did best in life felt good about themselves, and it seemed a short leap to conclude that the reverse must also be true: If successful people enjoyed high self-esteem, then high self-esteem would foster success. Students would do better if they had more self-esteem. Employees would work harder. Girls who felt inferior because of poor body image or math phobia would gain from self-esteem training.

By 1986, when California created a commission to bolster self-image as a statewide goal, the concept had become a pop-culture phenomenon. Celebrated in the media, in politics and in schools, self-esteem had become an end in itself—a commodity, like expanded memory for a personal computer, that could be installed in a do-it-yourself upgrade.

But now self-esteem is having image problems of its own.

Research is indicating that self-esteem is not in and of itself a strong predictor of success. Criminals and juvenile delinquents, it turns out, often have high self-esteem, using the traditional measurements. New political movements in education have turned on self-esteem and blamed it for students' failures in learning.

"Self-esteem became mixed up in a whole series of issues, and people wanted it over," said Arthur Levine, the president of Teachers College at Columbia University.

But self-esteem is by no means dead, researchers say. The United States' deep tradition of individualism guarantees that esteem or one of its many variants—from positive thinking to self-efficacy—will persist. What has changed is that self-esteem as an idea and a societal force has lost its unified champions and to a great degree its ability to be succinctly defined.

Like I.Q. tests and SAT scores, self-esteem has become but one gauge to indicate success in college or life.

"A dozen years ago, research was showing heavily positive things about high self-esteem," said Roy F. Baumeister, a psychology professor at Case Western Reserve University in Cleveland. "Since then, questions have been raised about the size of effects, the direction of effects and whether in fact it's a mixed blessing to even have high self-esteem."

Even before William James, the Harvard professor, philosopher and psychologist, invented the term self-esteem in the late 1800's, Americans have worshiped the concept of self. The will to do, to achieve, to improve, was stained into the culture along with its icons—Horatio Alger, Dale Carnegie, rags to riches. Other ideas of psychology, like alienation with its darker, more

*Reprinted with permission from *The New York Times*.

European nuances, never caught on in the United States, but bright-eyed, optimistic self-esteem did.

It was not until the 1960's, when new analytic tools were developed to measure self-esteem (particularly the Rosenberg Self-Esteem Scale, developed by Morris Rosenberg at the University of Maryland), that the idea really caught on. The scale, based on 10 questions, created what every academic craves—numerical measurability. At the same time, changes in society, especially the feminist movement, seized on the idea that low self-esteem among many girls and women could and should be raised through training.

But the zenith for self-esteem, often identified as the California project, was probably also the beginning of its undoing.

Confronted with the fact that self-esteem had become a goal for public schools and society, rather than a result of achievement, researchers realized they had no proof that the path of logic really worked that way. If you improved a person's self-image, did that translate into better behavior? By contrast, did life's losers really have poor self-esteem?

"The idea of self-esteem is so ingrained in our culture, it's presumed to be a real thing inside the human condition," said Timothy J. Owens, an associate professor of sociology at Indiana University. "But it got overblown on both ends—society's and the academy's."

In psychology, the idea has gained ground that there is no coherent self at all as people generally think of it, but rather a series of selves, like mirrors that reflect aspects of an individual's connection to the world.

"The critical notion of the unified self whose levels can be fixed—that idea has ended," said Kenneth Gergen, a psychology professor at Swarthmore College in Pennsylvania.

At the same time, the idea that high self-esteem is the exclusive province of those with admirable achievements has been rejected. Studies of gang members and criminals found their self-esteem—reinforced by peers or lawlessness—to be as high as that of any overachiever. Another study crushed the idea that welfare mothers became pregnant to boost self-esteem. Other studies found distortions in how self-esteem statistics had been gathered.

People, researchers concluded, are not the simple calculators of worth that the Rosenberg scale might indicate. Some people achieve great things in life while gripped by feelings of worthlessness. Others set low standards and feel great.

In the end, said Albert Bandura, a psychology professor at Stanford University, in his "Self Efficacy: The Exercise of Control" (1997, Freeman Press), "self-esteem affects neither personal goals nor performance."

Self-esteem became a cornerstone of the feminist critique of society beginning in the 1960's. But many feminist thinkers now say that trying to raise the self-esteem of girls and women may be self-defeating.

"Early feminism went in the direction of saying, 'Give every girl assertiveness training so she can get in there and compete,' and that made some sense at the time," said Judith V. Jordan, a psychologist at Harvard Medical School and director of training at the Stone Center for women's studies at Wellesley College. "Now we say, 'Why are we accepting that as the norm, why not change the norm?'"

Judith Butler, a professor of rhetoric and comparative literature at the University of California at Berkeley, added, "If you take an 11-year-old girl who's got failing self-esteem because her friends have name clothes or fancy haircuts, the real issue is to get that 11-year-old girl to think critically about how femininity is defined in the culture."

One of the paradoxes of self-esteem is that, in politics at least, conservatives are the people who came to oppose it. An idea that had been draped with all the trappings of individual self-improvement became instead associated with liberal values and political correctness, perhaps because of its surge to prominence in the unruly 1960's.

When education fell under attack in the 1990's because of declining achievement, said Professor Levine at Columbia, conservatives led the charge against "all the things that looked different, whether those things were elective curriculum or whole language, or self-esteem or multiculturalism."

The movement in education toward higher standards—visible everywhere from the New York City public schools to efforts in Washington to create national education standards—has shifted the emphasis toward achievement. The new view looks toward the world rather than the self, and toward results rather than motivation.

Richard F. Elmore, a professor of education at Harvard who has been working with the New York City schools, said that self-esteem—originally posited as a way to help underprivileged students—mutated instead into a kind of crutch that explained and even reinforced low achievement and low performance.

"For most teachers, self-esteem is a theory they invent to cover the fact that they have low expectations for kids," Professor Elmore said. By contrast, he said, the premise of an experimental program in District 2, which includes much of Manhattan's poor Lower East Side, is to train teachers to "accept no excuses" and to expect the same level of achievement that would be required of any middle-class student.

Deanna Burney, a former principal who helped put the District 2 program together, said, "We've led a lot of people astray about self-esteem—children feel good about themselves when they can read and write."

Professor Elmore said that while he remains optimistic about the standards movement, there is more talk than action around much of the nation. And few experts predict that self-esteem, whatever it may be called, will ever go away.

"It will come back," said Professor Butler at Berkeley. "As long as our society stays rooted in the individual, we'll be seduced again."

Questions

1. Use the concept of goals to explain how two people might both earn a B+ on an exam yet one feel positive about his- or herself afterward and the other negative.
2. What specific assumption about self-esteem is contradicted by data showing that successful criminals have high self-esteem? What specific assumption is contradicted by data showing that welfare mothers do not raise their self-esteem by having children?
3. How would you categorize the approach taken by Rosenberg to measure self-esteem (e.g., archive, observation, or self-report)? What are the advantages and disadvantages of this approach?
4. How would you categorize the type of research that initially led researchers to conclude that high self-esteem fosters success (e.g., true-experiment or correlational)? What cardinal rule of interpreting this type of data was ignored?
5. Compare the comments about self-esteem made by Jordan and Butler. Do they agree with each other? Can you extend either argument to suggest how to help boys with low self-esteem?

Reading 17

An Unusual Tool in Hiring the Right Person

Introduction

Psychologists are not the only professionals interested in measuring personality. During the past two decades a growing number of companies have begun using personality tests to help them with hiring decisions. Even some professional sports teams use personality measures when deciding which athletes to sign to contracts. The use of such tests is often controversial. For example, head coach Dan Reeves quit the NFL New York Giants in part because of disagreement with the owners over the use of personality tests in signing players.

Some of the personality tests used in industry are based on psychological theory and data. For example, well-standardized intelligence tests are often used. The most popular nonintelligence personality test used today is the Myers-Briggs, based on the work of Carl Jung, one of Freud's early disciples. Some personality tests, however, are of unknown validity. For example, self-report tests of honesty are often administered to job applicants, but it is not at all clear that these tests can distinguish honest people from dishonest people. Are dishonest people really likely to answer honestly questions about previous dishonest acts on a job application?

The next reading describes a new personality test on the market: the Kolbe index. The Kolbe is not a measure of honesty or intelligence. Designed by a former sociologist, the Kolbe claims to measure an aspect of personality untapped by previously available tests. What it does measure, creator Kathy Kolbe claims, is equally or more important in determining job success.

Penny Singer*
September 27, 1998

Twice a year, Ronald S. Rosbruch, an insurance executive, meets with a strategic business coach to discuss methods he can put into effect to improve the profitability and productivity of his company, National Retirement Planning Associates in White Plains.

"One day, we were talking about hiring," Mr. Rosbruch said, "how to find the right person, of course, but someone who would fit in with the team and stay for the long haul, which can be a problem in a strong job market."

Mr. Rosbruch's coach recommended that he use a personal assessment tool called the Kolbe Index, an alternative to personality tests, intelligence tests and other tests given in the workplace.

"It's very unusual, based on instinct," Mr. Rosbruch said. "My coach said he was using it in his own business, with terrific results."

Other users include dozens of major companies from Alaska Airlines to Chase Manhattan Bank to Intel to Xerox, all of which retain the Kolbe Company to administer Kolbe Indexes to their employees to help them define and work with their personal strengths.

"America is full of square pegs in round holes, and what we do helps employers match up the right person for the right job by harnessing the power of instinct, which brings out the best in people," Kathy Kolbe, founder and chief executive of the Kolbe Corporation, with headquarters in Phoenix, said in a phone interview from her office there.

Ms. Kolbe, a sociologist and a former journalist, has spent 30 years researching and testing her theory that instinct, not intelligence or personality, govern each individual's ability. She developed and refined the Kolbe concept over a 10-year period in which she analyzed the results of indexes from 20,000 people in all walks of life on five continents. She concluded that instincts fall into what she describes as four action modes: fact finders who have the instinct to probe and excel at evaluating and deliberating; follow-throughs who show the instinct to pattern and thrive when coordinating, planning and scheduling; quick starts who have the instinct to innovate and flourish when they originate, experiment and improvise, and implementors who show the instinct to demonstrate by constructing, repairing and crafting.

"Once you understand your instinct for taking action—and the four paths best for you to take—you can target your energy purposefully to achieve your goals," Ms. Kolbe said. "Then I developed diagnostic tools, the Kolbe Indexes, which give people a way to discover their mode of operations, literally a blueprint of their strengths as unique as a fingerprint. It tells people what they will or will not do, allowing them to understand their natural abilities and tap into their innate creativity."

---

*Reprinted with permission from *The New York Times*.

She said of her research: "I did it on a trial basis, gratis, for major corporations and Stanford University and the University of Chicago Business School. 'If I'm right,' I told them, 'this is the key to productivity.' Before I was satisfied it would work, I conducted more than 250,000 case studies."

And how successful were they? According to Ms. Kolbe's reliability studies, the Kolbe Indexes can predict behavior with uncanny accuracy, 82 percent of the time.

Ms. Kolbe's original approach to increasing productivity won her recognition in *Time* magazine in 1985 in its "Man of the Year" issue, in which she was cited, along with Ted Turner, as one of seven Americans who possess an abundant amount of the entrepreneurial spirit.

"I thought a cover story in *Time* would surely give a terrific boost to the business I was planning to start that month," she said. "But just before the launch, I was in a horrific car accident. A drunken driver hit us from behind, and for 18 months I was laid up. I couldn't even read or write."

When she recovered, Ms. Kolbe decided to take the Kolbe Index into the world.

"Late in 1986, I took a booth at a million-dollar round table convention in Chicago, which was attended by about 7,000 insurance executives," she said. "That was my test market. When people visiting our booth saw the results of the test, the product sold itself. In three days we had sold enough of our programs to finance the development of our software. And from that day to this, we've never advertised our products. Sales come from word of mouth."

The company has been profitable from the beginning. Now a multimillion-dollar business, the Kolbe Corporation sells its products in 23 countries. They range in price from $39.95 for the Kolbe Index—available at the Kolbe Web site at www.kolbe.com—up to $250,000 spent by *Fortune* 500 companies that use Kolbe to conduct everything from strategic planning to employee testing.

As for Mr. Rosbruch's experience, "Like most firms we looked at resumes, checked references and conducted interviews with job candidates, and our track record was so-so," he said. "When we got the Kolbe test, my partner, Jerry Harnick, and I answered detailed questions. Our skills matched the results exactly. So we arranged to use the test for new hires."

Mr. Rosbruch then gave the test to four qualified candidates for the position of executive administrator. "Nancy Imlej fitted the profile exactly of the person we were looking for," he said. "She rated very high in follow-up, strong on fact finding, reasonably good on quick start creative thinking and not so high on implementation. In this job, hands-on skills were not important."

Without the test, Mr. Rosbruch said, "maybe we wouldn't have been savvy enough to have chosen Nancy, but she has been a joy."

"We have 50 associates in this office who work on commission," he added, "and in 10 years we have had 4 different executive administrators, but we've never had such positive feedback across the board. Nancy's approval rate is in the 99th percentile; no other executive administrator ever came close. She has the ability to work with many personalities. A high level of productivity results when employees are doing what they are good at."

Ms. Imlej, who formerly worked in the international assignments department of International Business Machines and in the human resource sector of Sprint, applied for the job in Mr. Rosbruch's agency because she wanted experience at a small company.

"I'm very happy in the job," she said. "I wear a lot of hats, and every day is a little different. I also enjoy working with so many different personalities."

When asked if she worried about taking the test, she said: "Not at all. I was a psychology major in college, so I was intrigued by it. There were 36 multiple questions, no right or wrong answers. What I especially liked about it was that the results validated who I said I was and how I regard myself."

Questions

1. According to the Kolbe, what is the most important determinant of success in a specific job? What evidence do we have that the Kolbe actually measures what it purports to measure?
2. Did Rosbruch base his hiring of Imlej solely on the basis of her Kolbe score? Does this case study support the idea that action mode is more important than intelligence or personality in predicting success in a specific job?
3. Kolbe describes her four action mode types as "instincts" and the abilities that follow from them "innate." What evidence does she give to support the idea that action modes are biologically based and innate?
4. Why does Rosbruch believe that Imlej, his newly hired executive administrator, is so successful? Did these traits appear in her Kolbe profile?
5. What did Imlej like most about the Kolbe test? Is this quality true of most self-report tests? What are the implications of this for Rosbruch's initial decision to try the test on new hires?

Reading 18

On the Edge of Age Discrimination

Introduction

As experts on stereotypes and prejudice, social psychologists are increasingly asked to serve as legal experts in discrimination cases. Often their difficult task is to give an opinion about whether a particular person was hired or fired in part because of their group membership ("group membership" is used here broadly to mean one's racial group, gender group, religious group, etc.) or whether the hiring or firing decision was based entirely on the individual's merits. This task is complicated by the fact that employers are unlikely to admit on record that decisions are based on group membership. Thus a discrimination expert's job is to look for evidence that a company's management is systematically biased against certain groups. If a bias exists, then we are more likely to decide that specific employment decisions were based on group membership and so constitute illegal discrimination. For example, in the case of Hopkins *v.* Price Waterhouse, *psychologists argued and the court agreed that denying partnership to a woman because she is "too macho" constitutes gender discrimination because it insists that women match a cultural stereotype.*

The following reading examines another type of workplace discrimination: that based on age. On one side are corporations which argue that older employees are more often fired because of their higher wages or because they cannot keep up with changing technology. On the other side are career employees (some as young as their early 40s) who feel that firing them because of their wages or to avoid having to spend money to train them on newer technology amounts to age discrimination. These arguments are increasingly mediated by the courts, often with the help of a psychologist's expert testimony. As in the case of Hopkins *v.* Price Waterhouse, *their job is to look for indications that a company holds negative stereotypes against older workers or that cultural stereotypes of the aged (e.g., "you can't teach an old dog new tricks") cause them to be denied employment for no other reason than that they are older.*

Marianne Lavelle*
May 9, 1997

LaRue Simpson made $196,000 a year, played golf and owned thoroughbred racehorses before his life derailed, he contends, on the prejudice that does not discriminate by race, sex or class. A jury agreed that Simpson lost his job as a partner in the Cincinnati office of the accounting giant Ernst & Young because, at the age of 47, he was deemed too old by his firm.

With Ernst & Young prepared to ask the United States Supreme Court to overturn the $3.7 million verdict the accountant won in 1994, Simpson's age-discrimination case may prove to be a watershed for baby-boom professionals. Ernst & Young is fighting for the right of big law, accounting and consulting firms to decide whom they hire and fire as they always have—in the decorum of partnership agreements and without resort to unseemly (and unpredictable) lawsuits. But for Simpson and all who came of age at the birth of the civil rights movement, no course of action could be more proper than to imbue one's personal struggle with universal significance by taking it to court. His suit and others like it signal that, with all the vigor they once summoned to fight the Vietnam War, environmental pollution and repression of any kind, baby boomers are poised to attack an issue that is new only to them: how employers treat workers with long careers.

One indication of the trend is the series of record age-discrimination settlements the United States Equal Employment Opportunity Commission racked up in the past year, like Monsanto and Chevron's agreement to pay $18.3 million to 43 laid-off sellers of Ortho lawn-care chemicals—some of them as young as 41. The E.E.O.C. has no statistics yet to prove it, but at a meeting last June on age discrimination, the agency's chairman, Gilbert Casellas, noted the profusion of high-profile claims by workers at the younger end of this protected class. Even though, he might have added, those complaints require a person who should be in the peak years of a career to make an unabashed declaration of helplessness.

Simpson's case against Ernst & Young, for example, turns on a semantic issue: what is it to be a partner in a mammoth organization where you have no real decision-making power? And in a way, that question captures the loss of meaning, the slipping away of personal definition, that is the essence of age-discrimination cases. But Simpson was no weary Willy Loman. The 6-foot-5 former University of Kentucky basketball player struck a youthful pose in a local business journal in gym shorts three years before he was fired. And while Arthur Miller's tragic figure pleaded vainly to his boss, pay attention, as his work and life slipped from him, Simpson already has forced partnerships across the nation to take note. His case is a portent that the generation that glorified youth may revolutionize the value of age in the American workplace.

This year marks the 30th anniversary of the Age Discrimination in Employment Act, the Federal law protecting workers over 40 from not being hired or fired or from other work decisions based on age. Its passage was a little-noted flourish in the civil rights movement; racial and sexual equality attracted more attention on campuses then filled with students in the leading edge of the baby boom. The facts that one-half of the private-sector job openings at the time were advertised as closed to applicants over 55 and that one-quarter of those barred workers as young as 45 seemed far-off concerns.

Now that half of the labor force will be over 40 by the year 2005, there is no civil rights cause more relevant to baby boomers. Nor is there one more universal. If, for lack of kinship, any white man on a conservative career track could not fully appreciate the struggle of minorities and women against prejudice, statistics indicate that he will. More than 86 percent of age-discrimination complaints in the mid-1980's were filed by men, 79 percent by white-collar workers and 57 percent by managers, according to E.E.O.C. and other studies.

Three decades after the law's passage, older job applicants will be discriminated against one in four times when competing with younger applicants with the same credentials. Research in 1994 by the Fair Employment Council of Greater Washington for the American Association of Retired Persons showed that discrimination against older workers was about the same as that against African-Americans and Hispanics of all ages. The researchers also learned that older applicants could boost their chances only by hiding their age or emphasizing their youthful qualities. The worst strategy for an older applicant is to emphasize experience, stability, loyalty and maturity—stereotypical qualities, positive though they may be, associated with age. More than one in three such resumes were rejected outright.

Age-discrimination complaints filed annually before the E.E.O.C. or state and local employment agencies, the first step in any civil rights action, climbed from 24,813 in fiscal 1990 to a high of 32,145 in 1992. The agency calculates that employers in fiscal 1996 paid more than ever before in per-worker precourt resolutions of age-discrimination cases: $40.9 million to settle 1,931 cases. In those cases that make it to court, headlines suggest that employers are agreeing to multimillion-dollar payments. Most notably, the defense giant Lockheed Martin consented last November to pay $13 million to 2,000 nonunion employees who lost jobs in the old Martin Marietta Astronautics Group from 1990 to 1994.

Lockheed never admitted to bias, and many other managers argue that they are unfairly accused of age discrimination when decisions are purely economic. Regrettably, when a company has to reduce the workforce, it often has to remove lots of qualified people, says Ann Elizabeth Reesman, general counsel of the Equal Employment Advisory Council, an association of private-sector employers. That doesn't mean they are not any good or poor employees; it's just that the company doesn't have as many spaces. And that creates resentment for employees, especially long-term employees. Time and again, courts have ruled it legal for an employer to select workers with larger salaries for dismissal, even if they happen to be the older workers.

Kmart is defending itself against age-discrimination suits in part by arguing that dismissals of longtime store managers were legitimate business decisions. Kmart's managers, according to the argument, were once needed to keep inventory of clothing, toys, toaster ovens and other wares on store shelves. But the need for managers in whom to invest such trust evaporated with the introduction of scanners at checkout counters. Inventory decisions could be made by computer. Some of the ex-managers that now are charging the retailer with age discrimination are not yet in the over-50 population that as recently as the mid-1980's made up 82 percent of age-discrimination complainants.

Pamela Poff, a deputy general counsel at Paine Webber, says these cases are not warm and fuzzy as they once were, when employers were so ignorant of the law that they would simply tell workers they were too old. Today, she says, there are instances where, technologically or organizationally, a worker rises to a level where he or she no longer fits within the budgetary constraints of the department.

As a result, age bias has a different edge than racial or sex bias. Its victims are wounded not because of the skin or sex they were born with, but because of what they have become. For LaRue Simpson, pursuing an age-discrimination case meant defending in public what Ernst & Young used to justify his firing—his personal loans with firm clients, his thwarted ambition to become an office managing partner, his choice of serving small entrepreneurial clients that generated little revenue growth. The accounting firm still maintains that Simpson's firing had nothing to do with age. Ernst & Young is a firm that makes its hiring and retention decisions based on merit, says Kathryn A. Oberly, the firm's general counsel. That policy was followed in this case. She would not discuss it further pending the Supreme Court petition.

Baby boomers will learn, if they haven't already, that the age-discrimination claim that begins with the grandest clarion call for civil rights devolves—sooner or later—into the tinny noise of a trial over someone's job performance. Courts often clash over the resolution of such cases. A manager's comment to a diesel mechanic that at your age you cannot produce like you once could was ruled a neutral observation by a judge in Alabama; the Federal appeals court in Atlanta in 1994 said the remark was the very essence of age discrimination.

The Commonwealth Fund, a New York-based philanthropic group, financed research on whether worker performance declines with age for its Americans Over 55 at Work project—a program aimed at encouraging companies to attract, retrain and retain senior workers. A review of sociological literature showed that the only jobs for which performance appeared to decline with age were in manual labor, where many workers continue to be protected by union seniority rules. Researchers found no correlation between age and work quality for the group that lodges most age-discrimination complaints—supervisors and professionals. Skills actually appear to improve over the years for people in sales.

But skills that workers have perfected through experience may become less important with each passing year. The Commonwealth Fund noted that 48 percent of the executives surveyed see technology as important to the future of their business, but only 11 percent rated their older workers comfortable with new technology. Poff says that older workers may find themselves particularly vulnerable.

Jack Levin, a sociology professor at Northeastern University and the author of the 1980 book Ageism, argues that while laying off older workers may appear justifiable on the surface, such decisions are based on prejudice, nevertheless. Workers are told they lack certain qualities deemed absolutely essential, Levin says. "And I think you can summarize those qualities in one code word—versatility. The term is seen as a way of eliminating older workers based on a quality that they lack, as opposed to age. And I think many of those views are based on a stereotypical notion that you can't teach old workers new tricks."

The Commonwealth Fund concluded that not enough research has been done to gauge whether older workers are less trainable than younger employees. But researchers found that 90 percent of workers—young and old—will have to be retrained during their careers. And the payoff for training younger workers, who are more likely to hop to new jobs, may actually be less than for training older workers who stay put. However, employers have to craft training with care for older workers, who respond best to low-pressure training. Does a company's reluctance to invest in a program tailored to older workers constitute discrimination?

It will be a long time before the courts are asked to decide such a subtle issue. Most workers simply agree to cash settlements before volleys of charges and countercharges about their performance and trainability become public. The workers that make it to trial are those who find the paper trail, who hear the stray comment that suggests their cases, indeed, have something to do with youth and age. Exhibit A in the case of hundreds of Kmart store managers, expected to go to trial in Federal court in Atlanta later this year, is a videotaped news conference by Joseph Antonini, the former Kmart chief executive officer, at the unveiling of a new company logo in September 1990. "We are blessed with an officer group whose average age is slightly under 50 years," Antonini said. "Our middle management group . . . many of whom are here today, whose average age is 40, all are dedicated and committed to our strategies for the 90's."

For LaRue Simpson, the smoking gun was the agenda of Ernst & Young's management-committee meeting of Feb. 21, 1990, including the items Resignations and retirements—where we stand in the process and Comparison of partner ages in 1990. Ernst & Young compiled lists of the names, ages and years of service for every partner over 51. There also was a list of partners who had recently quit and their ages. Jesse Miles, Ernst & Young's co-chairman, said that management merely was gauging what positions would be vacated soon through retirement. As for the detail in which ages were noted, even for younger departing partners, Miles said, "The only way I could describe it is, being accountants, we like to total things."

Simpson's lawyer, Janet Abaray of Cincinnati, had another explanation. When Simpson and 98 other partners over 40 were fired, the company promoted 112 accountants under 40 to partnership. The salary saving alone was $5.5 million per year.

"Ladies and gentlemen, this is not a downsizing—this is an age-sizing," Abaray said at trial. Under questioning by Abaray, Miles had said, "We have to have bright capable young people joining us . . . on an annual basis in order to keep the lifeblood of the organization growing and growing and growing."

A jury's 1994 decision to award Simpson $3.7 million was a signal that baby boomers will not permit organizations like Ernst & Young to hire and fire as they have in the past. Casellas, the E.E.O.C. chairman, says: "While those in or just past the baby-boom years may be the targets of age discrimination, they may also be its final arbiters. Would a trial with a jury most likely made up of the middle-aged peers of those let go from Chevron have proved too risky for the company?"

Levin, the sociologist, sees in such stories hope that the present generation of older workers, by sheer force of numbers, can erode corporate prejudice against senior employees. The baby boomers have the cultural clout to significantly reduce age discrimination, he says. What an opportunity for them to take some of the influence, authority and marketplace power that they have and benefit everyone, especially themselves.

QUESTIONS

1. Corporate America is changing so quickly that the skills needed for success today are not the same as those needed 10 to 20 years ago. Give an example from this reading of how changing technology negatively affects older workers.
2. What stereotype does Levin think is responsible for a great deal of age discrimination in American companies?
3. Would you think it age discrimination if a company fired high-income workers to lower its payroll if this meant firing only senior (i.e., older) workers? Briefly defend your answer.
4. From what you know about LaRue Simpson's case in this reading, do you think he was unfairly discriminated against? What additional evidence, if any, would you want to have before making your decision?
5. Why does the AARP discourage older job applicants from describing themselves as having such positive qualities as maturity, experience, and stability? Use a social cognitive perspective in giving your answer.

Reading 19

Battered Women Face Pit Bulls and Cobras

Introduction

This next reading combines two of the more actively researched topics in both personality and social psychology: close relationships and aggression. The work reported in this article is exciting both for the findings reported and for the way the research was conducted. Research on close relationships is typically carried out in one of two ways. Academic psychologists conduct controlled studies on a large scale but normally study only young college students because this is the easiest group for them to study. Clinicians work with a much more diverse population and in greater depth than academic psychologists but normally rely more on case studies than large-scale systematic research. Clearly an ideal study would combine the depth and diversity of the clinical approach with the scale and experimental control of the academic approach. The research described in Jane Brody's article comes closer than most in achieving this ideal.

By studying a wide and diverse sample of couples in a systematic and controlled way, Dr. Gottman and Jacobson were able to identify two distinct types of abusive men. One type—which they call pit bulls—are highly emotional and have a tendency to lose control when angry. The other type—which they call cobras—are distinctly not emotional but are cold, calculating, even sadistic men who seem to enjoy controlling women through violence and the threat of violence. Although both personality types are prone to violence, the psychological underpinnings of their behavior differ dramatically. Because a cobra's violence is not caused by the same psychological problem as the pit bull's, a different solution is needed in each case. Only by recognizing the motives behind individual abusers can therapists and the legal system intervene effectively.

JANE BRODY*
MARCH 17, 1998

The cobra is a real snake in the grass, quiet and focused before striking its victim with little or no warning. The pit bull's fury smolders and builds, and once its teeth are sunk into its victim it won't let go. Men who batter women are either like cobras or pit bulls, say two professors of psychology at the University of Washington who have spent a decade studying violent marriages, and the distinction can make a difference in the severity of the harm they inflict, the ability of women to escape a relationship and the risks the women face if they do leave.

"Pit bulls are great guys, until they get into an intimate relationship," said Dr. Neil Jacobson who, with his colleague, Dr. John Gottman, elaborate on their study findings in a provocative new book, "When Men Batter Women" (Simon and Schuster, $25). "O.J. Simpson is a classic pit bull. Pit bulls confine their monstrous behavior to the women they love, acting out of emotional dependence and a fear of abandonment. Pit bulls are the stalkers, the jealous husbands and boyfriends who are charming to everyone except their wives and girlfriends."

Mr. Simpson was acquitted in 1995 of charges that he murdered his former wife, Nicole Brown Simpson, and one of her friends, Ronald L. Goldman, but was found to be responsible for the deaths in a subsequent civil trial.

Pit bulls, the psychologists say, monitor the woman's every move. They tend to see betrayal at every turn and it infuriates them. And when their anger explodes into violence, they seem to lose control.

Cobras, on the other hand, are often sociopaths. They are cold and calculating con artists relatively free of the trappings of emotional dependence but with a high incidence of antisocial and criminal traits and sadistic behavior, the researchers found. Cobras' violence grows out of a pathological need to have their way, to be the boss and make sure that everyone, especially their wives and girlfriends, knows it and acts accordingly.

When they think their authority has been challenged, cobras strike swiftly and ferociously, the study revealed. Although they do not lose control like the pit bulls, they are more violent toward their wives, often threatening them with a knife or gun. They are also likely to be aggressive toward everyone in their lives, including strangers and even pets, as well as friends, relatives and co-workers. Cobras are the ones who kill the cat as a warning to wives that if they fail to toe the mark, this could happen to them.

In their study of 201 couples, including 63 couples where the wives were repeatedly beaten and emotionally abused, the Seattle-based psychologists discovered an extraordinary physiological difference between the two types of batterers. They hooked up the couples to polygraphs that recorded characteristics

---

*Reprinted with permission from *The New York Times*.

like heart rate, blood pressure and skin resistance while the couples argued nonviolently in a laboratory setting about volatile issues in their marriages. The researchers noted that, as expected, the batterers they call pit bulls became physiologically aroused as their anger intensified, but, surprisingly, those labeled cobras calmed down internally as they became increasingly aggressive.

When the police are called in response to violence inflicted by a cobra, they are likely to find a highly agitated woman and a calm, controlled man who blames the incident on his wife, which sometimes results in the arrest of the wrong person, the researchers said.

Prof. Amy Holtzworth-Munroe, a psychologist at Indiana University in Bloomington, said that understanding the types of batterers and how they got that way should help in the development of more effective treatment programs, as well as efforts to prevent domestic violence.

"Right now, we take a one-size-fits-all approach to treatment," Dr. Holtzworth-Munroe said. "If we increase our understanding of subtypes, we could match treatment protocols to them."

The psychologists were prompted to explore this societal scourge in detail by compelling statistics and myths about domestic violence, and frustration with the general failure of therapy and the law to deal effectively with batterers. They point to estimates that two million to four million wives are severely assaulted each year by their husbands, and half of all murdered women are the victims of their husbands, ex-husbands, boyfriends or ex-boyfriends. The comparable statistic for murdered men is only 6 percent.

Yet, in only one of six battering episodes are the police called and in only 6 percent of severely violent episodes does the batterer end up in the criminal justice system.

For example, Dr. Jacobson said, when O.J. Simpson was arrested in 1989 and pleaded no contest to spousal abuse, "he was given a slap on the wrist." "If the laws were different and enforced differently, battered women would be much safer," he said. "If wife-beating was an automatic felony and the perpetrators had a mandatory jail sentence, women would have a chance to experience life without an abusive husband and an opportunity to formulate a safety plan to escape from the relationship."

Instead, Dr. Jacobson said, "batterers are often referred to treatment programs that don't work, and judges and therapists alike are conned by these men, especially by the cobras," who have little trouble convincing everyone, including their wives, that it is safe for them to return home.

Dr. Daniel Saunders at the University of Michigan School of Social Work said: "Treatment evaluation studies are still in their infancy. We're still trying to find out what works and in what types of men." The evidence thus far indicates that a combination of arrest, prosecution, fines and counseling works better than any one approach alone, he said.

In the Seattle study, the actions and responses among violent couples were compared with those of three other groups: equally unhappy but nonviolent couples, couples who exhibited some aggressive behavior but not enough to be classified as violent and happily married couples.

Participants were recruited through advertisements and were simply told the study would examine conflicts in marriage. When they joined the study, the couples completed extensive interviews and participated in laboratory-staged arguments that were videotaped and analyzed by independent observers who did not know how each couple was classified. A similar analysis was repeated two years later.

"There is occasional low-level violence in many marriages, with pushing or hitting with a pillow now and then out of frustration," Dr. Jacobson said. "This kind of behavior is found among about half of those who seek couples therapy, but it almost never develops into a battering relationship." Battering, the researchers insist, is not just a matter of physical aggression. Rather, Dr. Jacobson said, "it is aggression with the intent to control, subjugate or intimidate another human being, and in marriage it is almost always the man who fits this definition."

Once physical violence succeeds in intimidating the woman, it may even taper off, only to be replaced by a never-ending barrage of emotional abuse that is sufficient to remind the woman that the threat of physical violence is always present.

The two hallmarks of battering are fear and injury, Dr. Jacobson said. "Even though in 50 percent of the violent couples the wives were also violent, the men never showed fear in their voices or faces but the women virtually always were terrified and they get much more seriously injured," he noted.

Unlike the attacks by men, the violence of women is nearly always in response to battering by the man and is more self-defense than aggression, the researchers maintain. Yet, the men classified as pit bulls often profess that "they're the ones who are the victims in a violent relationship," Dr. Jacobson said. "O.J. Simpson said he felt like a battered husband. Cobras, on the other hand, know they are perpetrators and don't care."

While pit bulls may be easier to leave than cobras, in the long run they can be more dangerous. They are the ones who kill battered women on the courthouse steps when the women seek protection orders or divorces.

While the psychologists found that battered women are less likely to leave cobras, those who do escape face a shorter danger period because cobras generally stop trying to pursue them and go on to new conquests.

The histories of cobras and pit bulls also tend to differ. Cobras often had violent, traumatic childhoods, criminal records and a personal history of alcohol and drug abuse. Pit bulls, on the other hand, are less likely to have a history of delinquency or criminal behavior, but they are more likely than cobras to have had fathers who battered their mothers.

Drs. Jacobson and Gottman said their research shatters many prevailing myths about domestic violence. Contrary to the claims of batterers, their wives rarely do or say anything that would provoke a vicious attack in another kind of marriage. The same words and actions in a nonviolent marriage might trigger a disagreement or argument, but not a fist in the eye. Likewise, the psychologists state emphatically, there is nothing a woman can do or say to stave off or abort a battering episode. In many cases among their study subjects, when the woman tried to end an attack by leaving, the husband pursued her and intensified the beating.

Judging from the couples studied, the researchers concluded that battering almost never stops on its own. Although the frequency of physical attacks may diminish with time, in only one case did they stop altogether. Furthermore, even when physical attacks abated, emotional abuse continued and served to keep the wives intimidated and afraid. In fact, Dr. Jacobson said, emotional abuse can be even more damaging than physical abuse because the man is "always in her face, demeaning, degrading, humiliating, harassing and robbing her of her identity."

But in another myth-shattering discovery, the researchers found that a large number—38 percent—of women managed to escape from their abusive relationships within the two-year follow-up period. None, however, were the wives of cobras, who were terrified of their husbands' propensity to use lethal weapons. But at a subsequent contact five years after they entered the study, 25 percent of the cobra wives had also left their husbands. All told, 65 percent of the wives of violent men had left them at that point.

The researchers said those who left demonstrated extraordinary courage and resourcefulness, because it is upon leaving that the women face the greatest likelihood of being killed. But, as one woman who left said, "Death would be preferable to continue in this living hell."

Questions

1. To what percentage of battering episodes are police called? What percentage of these calls lead to any formal legal action? Taken together, what percentage of battering episodes result in formal legal action?
2. In what percentage of violent couples is the wife violent? Given that both men and women are often violent, why does Jacobson say that batterers are almost always men?
3. Cite three pieces of evidence from this reading used to argue that O.J. Simpson was a pit-bull type of abuser. Is this consistent with his having no prior arrest record?
4. What evidence do Jacobson and Gottman give to support their claim that there are two primary subtypes of batterers? Does this convince you that these are two distinct personality types?
5. How might a battered women's shelter, hot line, or therapist use the information presented in this reading to help women who are abused by these two different types of men?

Reading 20

Getting Serious About Adultery: Who Does It and Why They Risk It

Introduction

Every discipline that attempts to understand human behavior has been influenced by Darwin's theories of natural and sexual selection. And although some areas of psychology were more slow to incorporate evolutionary theories, it would be almost impossible now to find an area of psychology that did not take seriously the impact of selective pressures on human behavior. Surprisingly, evolutionary theories—with their emphasis on sexual selection—have only recently emerged in the one area where they would seem most directly applicable: dating and romantic relationships.

Within the general area of romantic relationships, recent events (i.e., President Clinton's relationship with Monica Lewinsky and the subsequent string of admissions by congressmen of similar affairs) have focused public attention on the issue of marital infidelity. Although it is difficult to estimate accurately the incidence of infidelity among American's married couples, our best estimates are that at least 25% of married men and 18% of married women will have at least one extramarital affair. Psychologists would like to understand why so many people fail to keep their wedding vow of monogamy, and evolutionary theories are among the contending explanations. In the following reading, Buss and Shackelford extend an earlier argument that selection pressures affected men and women differently such that women are more selective than men about whom they have sex with. Consequently, we should predict different patterns of infidelity among men and women.

Michael Normal*
July 4, 1998

Bertrand Russell, the wide-eyed British logician, simply couldn't understand why people got so worked up about a little bit of dallying, why they seemed unable to "distinguish sexual intercourse from marriage as a procreative partnership" and simply wink at the former and carry on with the latter.

He blamed the "psychology of adultery" for many of the sexual woes of society, the misery, as he put it, that usually follows what the French call liaison intrigue.

Views about sex and marriage, of course, are complicated and often contradictory. Americans may be moralistic and conventional (to use Russell's judgment) but they are also tolerant. In the context of a good economy, for instance, polls show that Americans seem to care little about whether their President is chronically concupiscent. And perhaps this ambivalence, in part, explains why tens of millions of American men and women have had extramarital affairs or know well someone who has. Still, there is limited data and only a small amount of research dedicated specifically to infidelity.

"More than any other human behavior, adultery is cloaked in secrecy," said David Buss, a psychologist at the University of Texas at Austin.

Nevertheless, generations of cultural critics, writers, philosophers, clerics, politicians and so on have been trying to explain adultery, and now social scientists have joined them. So far they have assembled only a relatively small body of specific data, and although that work is often colored by ideology, personal experience and research samples too small to be conclusive, the ideas that are beginning to emerge from these efforts offer a fascinating peek at our roiling emotions, biological appetites and libidinous itches.

The research falls roughly under two disciplines: social demography (who does it) and psychology (why they take the risk).

One of the most reliable statistics on adultery comes from the National Opinion Research Center at the University of Chicago. In 1992 the center sent hundreds of interviewers to gather data on the sexual conduct of Americans in the National Health and Social Life Survey. In a face-to-face survey of 3,432 adults born from 1933 to 1974, researchers asked: "Have you ever had sex with someone other than your husband or wife while you were married?"

A quarter of the married men in the United States and a sixth of the married women reported having at least one extramarital affair.

Like all statistics, the data invited different interpretations. The sociologists who conducted the study wrote in "Sex in America: A Definitive Survey" that the figures show a "picture of an essentially monogamous America"

---

and that "each individual spends most of his or her life with only one partner." Although marriage and divorce rates may seem alarming, those in serial relationships tend to be faithful "as long as the marriage is intact."

More striking, perhaps, is this: Almost 90 percent of the men surveyed and 94 percent of the women believed that extramarital sex was "always wrong" or "almost always wrong." In other words, the overwhelming majority of Americans either practiced monogamy or aspired to it.

"People in the United States almost universally think adultery is wrong even while they are doing it," said John Gagnon, a professor of sociology at the State University of New York at Stony Brook and one of the authors of the Chicago study.

But the same data also suggest a different skein. The Chicago ratios applied to today's population mean that some 19 million American men and 12 million American women have entwined at least once outside the marriage bed. "That's a helluva lot of people being unfaithful," said Todd K. Shackelford, an assistant professor of psychology at Florida Atlantic University.

What is more, many social scientists think the Chicago percentages are low. "Can we really expect people to be honest about such a critical, life-changing event?" Mr. Shackelford asked. And his clinical colleagues agree. "We have to realize that if someone is going to lie to their husband or wife, they sure as hell are going to lie to a poll taker," said Frank Pittman, a psychiatrist in Atlanta who writes widely on adultery. "You're asking them to expose the worst thing they ever did."

Experts divide even more when they are asked why people commit adultery. In the last two decades, some social scientists have insisted that all human behavior is a product of millennia of adaptation, and increasingly human sexual behavior, including adultery, is being examined through an evolutionary lens.

When Helen Fisher, an anthropologist, began to study adultery in the 1980's, she found that "there exists no culture in which adultery is unknown, no cultural device or code that extinguishes philandering."

Intrigued by the conundrum of human mating behavior—the preference for monogamy alongside the pervasive fact of "extra-pair copulation"—Ms. Fisher, a research associate at the Center for Human Evolutionary Studies at Rutgers University, recently wrote a paper in which she contends that the neurochemical circuitry of the brain accounts for a person's sex drive, sexual attractiveness and sense of attachment.

"The human animal," she said in an interview, "is built to love more than one person at a time. In other words, we are capable of feeling long-term attachment while we feel attracted to someone at the office or the club or on the street. We have neurocircuitry that can lead us to adultery, and we have neurocircuitry that allows us to say 'no' to adultery."

As Mr. Buss describes this idea, across evolutionary history men and women "have evolved short-term and long-term mating strategies." Each strategy has benefits for the species. Long-term mating, or monogamy, as it might be called, aids "pair-bond maintenance," or in acquiring the basic necessities of life, and child-rearing. The short-term mating strategy is adultery.

In men, Mr. Buss says, this is the evolutionary impulse or need to reproduce, to mate with as many different women as possible to make sure the bloodline, and thus the species, survives. In women, however, the evolutionary urge is harder to explain, given the risks: the loss of a mate-provider and all the resources that go with him. "The big mystery," as he puts it, at least in evolutionary terms, is, "what do women get out of it?"

And here he has developed several theories, among them:

- The resources hypothesis. A lover may supply extra food or better protection than a woman's long-term mate.
- The genetic diversity hypothesis. Here, said Mr. Buss, "a woman can produce genetically variable offspring if she has them with genetically different males," or, In Mr. Buss's words, "it's like hedging your bets in the stock market by diversifying your investments."
- The mate-switching hypothesis. Women "might use affairs if they have a mate who has fallen down, not providing resources or hurting the children."

Mr. Buss's colleague, Mr. Shackelford, says that "when the benefits are much higher than the costs, both men and women are wonderfully good at committing adultery." He quickly added with some heat: "Now, that doesn't make it all right. I'm married and don't want my wife to be adulterous. I don't care if there are evolved mechanisms or not."

Therapists Ask Which Comes First

Both Mr. Shackelford and Mr. Buss caution that a lot of their work is theoretical and speculative. And some prominent scholars have questioned the whole premise of evolutionary psychology, dismissing much of the work as hypotheses without a shred of proof. Among those who study human sexuality, particularly clinicians and therapists, the notion that infidelity has somehow evolved as adaptive behavior holds little weight.

Neil Jacobson, a professor of psychotherapy research and director of the Center for Clinical Research at the University of Washington, is designing a major study to answer one of the fundamental questions among clinicians. "We want to know to what extent affairs are being caused by existing marital problems or to what extent the affair caused marital problems that did not exist," he said.

The sociologists who conducted the University of Chicago sex survey feel they have answered this question. Edward O. Laumann, the George Herbert Mead Distinguished Service Professor in the department of sociology, said the data he and his colleagues collected in 1992 clearly showed that people get into adultery when the marriage is troubled.

But Mr. Jacobson is not so sure. "We don't want to let the lore from the culture or the clinical lore lead us into thinking we know the answer," he said. So he wants to know: Did marital trouble lead to the affair or did the affair cause the trouble? Do men and women react differently to the news? What makes an adulterer? (The popular wisdom is that women dally for love or emotional satisfaction, men for sex or pure pleasure.)

In Atlanta, Frank Pittman, a psychiatrist who has written often on the subject in books and magazines, estimates that he has treated some 5,000 couples in the last 38 years. Lately he has noticed "women seem to be having more affairs than they did 20 years ago, 10 years ago," in part because as they travel more for work, they have more opportunities for affairs far from home, he said.

"I've also started to see a few female philanderers," he added, "married women who have casual affairs in what used to be the old male pattern of find 'em, bed them, forget them, the kind of sport men used to brag about."

Testing the Effects of Baby Boomers

Pepper Schwartz, a sociology professor at the University of Washington, is trying to test the notion that the baby boom generation, the cohort that began "the sexual revolution," came into adulthood with different cultural and moral values from their parents'. Using data from other studies and some 300 interviews she plans to conduct, she hopes to chart the details of baby boom love, sex and marriage, including extramarital amourettes.

Whatever she and the others discover, the subject of adultery will probably hold the species' collective curiosity for a very long time. Ever since Homer set Odysseus wandering and surrounded the faithful Penelope with suitors, adultery has been a major theme in Western culture. "It has fascinated people," said Professor Schwartz, "because anyone who lives a hidden life is fascinating. We're shocked and fascinated when we find out what is really going on: that lovely couple down the street is having an affair with that other lovely couple down the street."

Questions

1. If there are 60 students whose parents are married in your class, on the basis of the Chicago survey how many of 60 fathers have had an affair? How many of the 60 moms? Is your interpretation of the frequency of affairs closer to Gagnon's or Shakelford's?

2. Shackelford argues that people underreport extramarital affairs because it is the worst thing they have ever done. Is there evidence that people would consider an affair the worst thing they ever did?
3. Why does Buss think it harder to explain why women have affairs than why men do? Can his theory explain the similar incidence of marital infidelity among men and women?
4. What trend has Pittman noticed in women's infidelity over the past 20 years? Is this consistent or inconsistent with the evolutionary explanation of gender differences in affairs?
5. Jacobson is conducting a study to find out whether infidelity precedes or follows marital unhappiness. How will this help him in his debate with Buss and Shackelford?

Section V
Psychopathology and Its Treatment

Reading 21

On the Fringes of the Bell Curve, the Evolving Quest for Normality

Introduction

Our final readings center around abnormal behavior and our attempts to change it. The first reading in this section addresses one of the most fundamental questions in psychotherapy: How do we classify a person or behavior as abnormal? This may at first seem like an obvious or unimportant question, but as you will see, trying to define normal and abnormal is both greatly complex and critically important. The definition of "normal" is important because classifying a person or behavior as "abnormal" implies a moral failing. Under earlier versions of the Diagnostic and Statistical Manual *(the classification system of the American Psychological Association), homosexual behavior was classified as an abnormal behavior. Psychologists thus treated homosexuality as a disease and homosexuals as sick. The current* Diagnostic and Statistical Manual *does not classify homosexuality as abnormal. This change in classification was not based on empirical data as much as a shift in society's acceptance of alternative sexual orientations.*

This example reveals how easy it is to define "abnormal" on the basis of cultural prejudices. But our goal as psychologists is to avoid such prejudicial categorization as much as possible. A more objective classification might be based on frequency, with common behaviors and traits classified as normal and uncommon ones as abnormal. The problem with this approach can be easily seen in the examples of philanthropist

Mother Teresa and serial killer Jeffery Dahmer. Both personalities are highly unusual but most people would not think both needed therapy. Yet our instinct to want to change Dahmer but not Teresa is based on our culture's views about murder and self-sacrifice. In other words, we have returned to using subjective biases as our criteria in deciding what behavior should be modified with therapy. These thorny issues are not easily resolved, and you will probably find that the following reading suggests more questions than answers.

GINA MARANTO*
MAY 26, 1998

At first glance it seems an item that might vaguely interest furniture sellers or interior designers: Before the dismantling of the Berlin Wall, psychotherapists in the German Democratic Republic practiced in rooms fitted with circles of chairs; now they do so in rooms furnished with a couch.

Yet this interior redecorating is evidence of a major renovation of psychology, said the sociologist Christine Leuenberger, who has extensively interviewed therapists in eastern Germany in the last few years. Between 1950 and 1989, she said, virtually everyone receiving psychological treatment in the German Democratic Republic was consigned to group therapy.

Today, one analyst told Ms. Leuenberger, it "is exactly the opposite." Unification caused a shift, such that, by the analyst's estimate, 96 percent to 97 percent of patients now receive one-on-one treatment, often psychoanalysis.

Ms. Leuenberger was among a dozen scholars who presented papers recently at a Cornell University workshop titled, "Making People: The Normal and Abnormal in Constructions of Personhood," which was sponsored by the university's Department of Science and Technology Studies and underwritten by the National Science Foundation. Amid flowering trees on a bluff overlooking Cayuga Lake, about 30 professors, post-doctoral fellows, graduate students and undergraduates spent three days discussing the diverse ways in which science and medicine, along with legal systems and states, shape society's notions of who and what people are, who is sick and who is well.

Far from being inherent in nature, the categories normal and abnormal have been crafted over the last 150 years or so. Concepts regarding what is normal and abnormal have had a major impact on modern life, shaping scientific and medical research and determining the sort of education and psychological treatment people receive, among other things.

Normality has been subject to redefinition as a result of various pressures, including economic ones. For example, as Ms. Leuenberger noted, the changes in treatment styles and theoretical approaches in eastern Germany have also altered convictions about what is normal development and a psychologically healthy person. Therapists told her that though they formerly fostered "socialist," group oriented, personalities they now are concerned with helping clients achieve independence and autonomy, qualities that clients also seem to believe are necessary to their noncollectivist, market-economy oriented lifestyles.

Until the 1840's, normal simply meant "standing at right angles; perpendicular," according to the *Oxford English Dictionary.* Starting in the mid-Victorian years, and especially after the British adventurer and scientist Francis Galton put forth the principles of eugenics, the so-called science of improving the human species by breeding, the term normal came to be applied widely to the human body and psyche. The Belgian astronomer and statistical pioneer Adolphe Quetelet had found, for example, that the heights of any group of people tended to array themselves neatly about an average value. Galton saw in this symmetrical distribution of values around a mean, or "normal curve," a portrait of society.

Comfortably clumped under the dome of the bell-shaped curve sat the mass of humanity, while out at the narrow lip lay, on one side, geniuses and, on the other, the "feeble-minded."

At the Cornell workshop, the normal curve was a historical reference and a prop. Prof. John Carson, who organized the workshop for the university's Department of Science and Technology Studies, took a copy of "The Bell Curve," the much-debated 1994 best seller by Charles Murray and Richard J. Herrnstein, and used its lurid cover illustration of the curve as a visual aid. The book was used by several other speakers, who by the end of a long day could draw a laugh just by waggling it.

The joke had a serious subtext: the British historian Roger Smith, author of the "Norton History of the Human Sciences" (1997), said in his presentation on the life sciences that reference to the normal has great force precisely because it so seamlessly joins description, which in the scientific view is value neutral, and evaluation, which entails making judgments about worth or moral status.

But what of the abnormal? The French philosopher Georges Canguilhem in his classic work, "The Normal and the Pathological" (1943), and others have argued that the process by which science established the concept of normality made it no longer possible to view the pathological or abnormal as a qualitatively distinct state.

In effect, the abnormal no longer lay on the other side of an unfordable gorge. Instead, with the bell curve, the very concept of the normal was a kind of bridge to the abnormal.

Pathological states were part of a measurable continuum. If a ruler were held up to human beings, mere units of difference marked the distance from the ordinary to the extraordinary.

At the workshop, Dr. Carson turned Dr. Canguilhem's analysis around, proposing that "the normal did not so much create the abnormal as the reverse." This happened, he said, precisely because scientists in the early 1900's found it relatively easy to characterize and test for abnormality.

American psychologists signed on in droves to the enterprise of identifying so-called idiots, imbeciles and morons, while an array of laws and institutions sprang up to isolate and tend to such persons. Issues regarding ostensibly abnormal and subnormal members of society became a major topic of concern in the news media, in political forums and in drawing rooms. As Dr. Carson noted, Congress was presented with six bills having to do with the "abnormal classes" in 1902 alone.

But the abnormal tended to creep toward the normal. Take, for instance, the case of the fingerprint. At the workshop, Dr. Simon Coles, of Rutgers University, traced attempts by 19th-century anthropologists to set up a system by which the fingerprint could be read as a distinguishing mark of a criminal type. If, as in the plan of the Italian psychologist Cesare Lombroso, long fingers were the dead giveaway of a thief, so, too, whorls and other patterns on the skin might be an inescapable biological indicator of an outlaw.

Work on the front lines of criminology, like that of the Parisian police official Alphonse Bertillon, undermined this effort to link fingerprints and criminality. Instead, the fingerprint proved to be a normal attribute, albeit one whose seemingly infinite variability allowed it to be used as a means of identifying individuals, including those who might have handled objects at the scene of a crime.

Even as abnormality began to be considered more normal, there remained one class of people beyond all bounds: the insane. Madness had "no fixed address on the continuum running from the normal to the pathological," the sociologist Joel Eigen of Franklin and Marshall College in Lancaster, Pa., said in a paper delivered at the workshop.

Dr. Eigen detailed how even these outsiders were assigned a conceptual home on the same street as everyone else, oddly enough through the legal system. The testimony in British courts of so-called mad doctors, who were emerging as legal experts on insanity, from 1760 to 1853 tended to undermine legal standards regarding what a normal person was. Over several decades, by increasingly exercising their expertise to describe defendants as impaired or sick, rather than evil, mad doctors slowly normalized states of consciousness "that the law had historically typified as partial insanity and barred from the courtroom only a half-century earlier." Essentially, these physicians asserted their professional authority and created a new type of person to be reckoned with legally.

So too, contemporary psychiatry has created a bewildering array of types. Whereas psychologists could deploy only a handful of terms categorizing abnormal individuals at the beginning of the century, the fourth and most recent version of their Diagnostic and Statistical Manual lists about 260 forms of mental illness.

In his talk, Kenneth Gergen, a professor of psychology at Swarthmore College in Pennsylvania, contended that while these terms have been positive insofar as they have taken the moralism out of society's attitudes toward "deeply problematic people," they can also be viewed as part of a "cycle of progressive infirmity." As the professional labels move out of the psychotherapeutic community and become part of common language, people become less able to name and deal with their problems. Meaning is lost as phrases like "feeling blue," give way to psychological jargon. As more people seek professional help, the ranks of psychotherapists grow, and so the technical terminology proliferates.

Instead of accommodating oddly behaved people, society now identifies them in order to segregate them. Said Dr. Gergen, "A kid who doesn't sit still in class gets taken out and becomes infirm, diseased"—a child who has attention deficit disorder.

Meanwhile, those in the therapeutic, pharmacological and insurance industries have an increasing economic stake in the existence of such abnormal people. Dr. Gergen asked: "At what point does it stop? The latest addictions added to the DSM-IV have to do with eating, work, exercise, religion and sex." Engagement in life itself, he suggested drily, has become a diagnosable mental illness.

Dr. Gergen expressed concern about the way in which other values, ideas and voices get pushed aside by the whole psychological enterprise. "By locating disease within individual minds, we not only fail to consider the broader social context in which the problems are occurring," he said, "but we also generate a world picture in which people are fundamentally separate."

After the workshop, strains of music, played on a non-Western scale, drifted up the hill. A gray sieve of clouds hung over the valley. Down-slope, in front of an imposing stone hall built in what Dr. Smith, a professor at the University of Lancaster, had called "English-insane-asylum style," a woman in tulip-red silk pajamas danced on a raised stage that had been set up for Earth Day festivities. Half a dozen people stood, slickers on, umbrellas up, watching her angular dance in the steady rain. It seemed an extremely normal thing to do.

QUESTIONS

1. How did the use of fingerprints to identify criminals change from their initial conception as consistent with Lombroso's work to their use today?
2. Describe the normal curve. What area of scores under this curve are considered "normal"? What makes a person "abnormal" using this definition? Would Albert Einstein be considered abnormal using this definition?
3. How has the reunification with the West affected the definition of psychological normality in East Germany?
4. Using the bell curve concept of normality, do normal and abnormal people differ qualitatively or quantitatively? What does this imply about the difference between a so-called normal individual and a clinically depressed person?
5. What does Gergen mean by criticizing attempts to locate disease within individual minds? What alternative is he suggesting? Use the example of attention-deficit disorder in giving your answer.

Reading 22

As Drugs for Depression Multiply, So Do the Hard Questions

Introduction

Depression might not be the prototypical psychological disorder, but it is by far the most common. Depression is the fourth most commonly diagnosed mental or physical disorder and the first most commonly diagnosed disorder among women. In their lifetime, 1 in 5 women will exhibit the symptoms of clinical depression. In order to treat depression, psychologists have long used both psychotherapies (e.g., psychoanalysis or cognitive/behavioral therapy) and medical therapies (e.g., electroshock and drug therapy). But in the decade of the 1990s, the drug Prozac and other serotonin reuptake inhibitors (SRIs) became the most common form of treatment.

But Prozac is not turning out to be the miracle cure it was hoped (and hyped) to be. Approximately 30% to 40% of depressed people are unaffected by this class of drugs. And many of those that initially benefit from SRIs find the benefits diminish over time or are forced to give them up because of intolerable side effects, including loss of sexual interest and gastrointestinal pain. The failure of SRIs to cure Americans of depression (depression is more common today 10 years after Prozac than ever before) is causing psychologists to reexamine some difficult questions about this mood disorder.

Among the questions still unanswered about depression are the relative contributions of biological and cultural factors in the development of the disorder. And why do these factors conspire to affect women more than men? Equally puzzling is why people may respond to one SRI but not another that is psychoactively almost identical. And why do some people fail to respond to any drug at all? It is hoped that by finding answers to these questions, psychologists will be able to develop more powerful remedies for depression, the most common psychological disorder.

Natalie Angier*
June 22, 1997

Cheryl F. is a 37-year-old therapist in Rhode Island who has spent the last few years struggling to tame her own emotional dybbuks. In the early 1990's, she received a diagnosis of dysthymia, a chronic, low-grade depression that lingers for two years or longer. Unlike full-blown clinical depression, which can knock you into an agonized state of catatonia, dysthymia (pronounced dis-THIGH-mee-a) steals life in day-size pieces.

Cheryl, who spoke on condition of anonymity, managed to get to work each morning and to mime the behaviors of productive citizenry. But her mood was ever the color of dust and her self-esteem its texture. Her marriage was faltering. Her sleep was fitful. Finally, her psychiatrist suggested that she take antidepressant medication, and though she balked—Am I that sick? she asked, in shame and shock—she decided to give it a try.

"It" became "them" as she began the increasingly widespread practice of what might be called drug dipping—migrating from one psychiatric medication to the next. Her story exemplifies the promise and frustrations that characterize the treatment of mood disorders in women, who suffer from depression in much greater numbers than men. It can also be taken as a cautionary note—make that a cautionary fugue—against perky testimonies to the miracles of modern treatments for depression.

Now that psychiatric drugs are no longer reserved for severe mental illness, and in light of vigorous campaigns to portray depression as a condition similar to high blood pressure or diabetes, thistly new questions have arisen. One is how to distinguish between a mild case of depression that lasts for years but still ranks as a "disease," and an inborn temperament called the depressive personality type that is "normal"—if unpleasant—and probably not amenable to fixing.

Moreover, even as many researchers now argue that depression is a recurring and insidious condition requiring prolonged maintenance treatment, often with drugs, they admit that the long-term effects of antidepressants are unknown. And though the new antidepressants like Prozac and Zoloft are considered safer than their predecessors, they have side effects that, it turns out, can worsen over time.

Depressive disorders exert an enormous psychic, physical and financial toll on society. One recent study found that the annual cost of depression in the United States, as a result of early death, lost days of work and lowered productivity, is at least $43 billion.

Questions and worries about depression in its myriad guises are of particular concern to women. By one estimate, about 25 percent of women display at least some symptoms of dysthymia or mild depression at any given time, which is hardly surprising given that the symptom menu includes low self-esteem and fatigue.

In a survey published last year of 38,000 people in 10 countries around the world, Dr. Myrna M. Weissman of Columbia University's College of Physicians and Surgeons and her international collaborators found that, while the overall lifetime rates of depression vary widely across countries, women universally are at two to three times the risk of the illness when compared with their male counterparts.

The reasons for women's greater vulnerability to depressive disorders remain murky and subject to perhaps predictable debate over how much to attribute to culture, how much to biology. Some experts argue that the cross-national evidence indicates an innate female susceptibility.

"I think there is no question that males and females are different biologically, and that this has something to do with the expression of emotion and the vulnerability to depression," said Dr. Weissman.

Yet efforts to identify the source of that predilection have proved far more intricate than a matter of the old biological bugaboo, "female hormones." Dr. Mary F. Morrison, an assistant professor of psychiatry and medicine at the University of Pennsylvania, points out that attempts to correlate depression with levels of estrogen or progesterone in premenopausal women have failed.

Beyond sex hormones, women and men may differ in their capacity to generate and metabolize serotonin, the neurochemical most strongly implicated in depressive disorders. As reported last month in the journal *Proceedings of the National Academy of Sciences,* researchers from McGill University in Canada used brain-imaging scans to study serotonin production in a group of healthy men and women. They found that, on average, the men synthesized 52 percent more serotonin than the women did. But what those results mean nobody knows: some studies suggest that having too much serotonin floating freely through the brain is as bad for mood as is a deficit.

Others emphasize the sociocultural aspects of depression and dysthymia, pointing out that those who suffer from depressive disorders may have reason to be dissatisfied with their lives. Indeed, whatever risks for depression women may inherit, life bequeaths plenty of new ones. Dr. Martha L. Bruce, an associate professor of sociology and psychiatry at Cornell University Medical College, has found that one of the biggest risk factors for depression is poverty, which is overwhelmingly a female affliction. Sex abuse in childhood is another major risk factor, and girls are sexually abused more often than boys.

"I don't think we're looking at depression from a social perspective enough," said Dr. Carol Landau, a clinical professor of psychiatry and human behavior at Brown University School of Medicine. "Should we be working 14 hours a day at the office and 7 hours at home? I don't think so. I've seen women whose antidepressants medicate their symptoms so they don't challenge the larger system. Would I take their medication away? Absolutely not. Should we challenge the system anyway? Absolutely."

In wrestling with her malaise, Cheryl turned first to the grand vizier of antidepressants, Prozac. But her liver couldn't tolerate the drug and she had to stop. She also took an antidepressant called Desyrel to treat her sleep disorder, and gave it up once the drug corrected her sleep patterns.

When the birth of her daughter left her with postpartum depression (she did not take any antidepressant drugs while pregnant), she tried a new antidepressant, Serzone, but found it had no effect. Her dysthymia persisting, she tried Paxil, a chemical cousin of Prozac. Success. She began to feel stronger, less irritable, better able to hammer away at her problems through psychotherapy. She might have chosen to stay on Paxil indefinitely except for one problem: she was getting fat. Contrary to initial hopes that the serotonin-based drugs could serve as weight-loss aids, they seem to do the opposite.

As of last month, she had weaned herself from the medication and was feeling fine. All things considered, she says her experience with antidepressants has been positive. Yet she says the drugs are "not curative, just palliative," and that genuine transformation, for her, can happen only through psychotherapy.

Others concur with that assessment. Dr. Gary Y. DeNelsky, a psychologist at the Cleveland Clinic, has shown with his colleagues that highly structured and task-oriented forms of psychotherapy like cognitive behavioral therapy and interpersonal therapy work as well as antidepressants in treating all forms of depression.

Unfortunately, said Dr. Robert M. A. Hirschfeld, chairman of the department of psychiatry at the University of Texas Medical Branch in Galveston, many of those who could be successfully treated never get any care. As he and other members of a consensus panel reported earlier this year in the *Journal of the American Medical Association,* only about a third of people displaying such symptoms of depression as sleep disturbance, weight change, inability to concentrate and relentlessly blue mood receive adequate treatment for their illness.

"Even though the media like to say that everybody is on Prozac," Dr. Hirschfeld said, "in fact, far too few people are on Prozac and other antidepressants."

Yet the success rate for any of the current medications is only about 60 percent, Dr. Landau said. For the other 40 percent, switching to a different drug or strategy might work—or it might not. As it turns out, an unknown subpopulation of apparent depressives will never find mental balm in a medication because they are not really "ill," they are just born crabs.

One way of telling is to look for the physical signs of depression, like insomnia, appetite changes and fatigue, said Dr. Larry J. Siever, a professor of psychiatry at Mount Sinai Medical Center in New York. "My rule of thumb is, the more bodily symptoms you have, the more responsive you'll be to antidepressants."

Distinguishing between dysthymia and disagreeableness is often a retrospective matter, doctors say—that is, if the drugs work and you feel better, then you must have been mildly depressed. Otherwise, welcome to the problem of being yourself.

There is also a nasty little secret of psychopharmacology: the people who benefit most from these drugs are those most likely to report serious side effects. For the Prozac-style drugs, one of the commonest downsides is loss of libido and orgasmic capacity. Another is the Florida effect: antidepressants may iron out your moods, but after a while some people miss the changing of their emotional seasons.

Because antidepressants are highly profitable, with global sales estimated at $6 billion a year and rising, pharmaceutical companies are striving to develop medications with more good effects and fewer bad ones. But for now, such designer drugs remain in the realm of fantasy, along with calorie-free food and no-sweat fitness. Nothing about depression is simple or smooth: not its cause, not its course and not its care.

Questions

1. What does Cheryl mean when she says the antidepressants she took were "just palliative"? What does this suggest about the cause of depression?
2. What percentage of women can be classified as dysthymic at any given time? On what symptoms is this diagnosis based? Could these symptoms be caused by something other than mood disorder?
3. Why does finding that women suffer from depression more than men in many different countries suggest that biological differences between the sexes is responsible?
4. What sociocultural factors might explain greater female depression in this culture? Can these same factors also explain the cross-national findings of greater female depression?
5. Siever says that when antidepressants do not help someone's mood, the person is not depressed but just a naturally unhappy person. Do you find this argument compelling? Why or why not?

Reading 23

New Theories of Depression Focus on Brain's Two Sides

Introduction

The previous reading chronicled the failed promise of the last great hope to find a cure for depression (serotonin reuptake inhibitors), raising interesting questions about the nature of depression. The next reading describes two exploratory treatments that their developers hope will initiate the next wave in treatment for depression, proposing some interesting answers.

Because the theories and treatments discussed in Sandra Blakeslee's article are quite experimental, consider each claim carefully before accepting it. It is, of course, always important to approach new ideas with a certain amount of healthy skepticism, but this is especially true when ideas are very new and not yet well tested. New treatments must be explored in carefully controlled studies that control for the potential interference of placebo and Hawthorne effects, which occur when people in a psychological study feel better not because a particular treatment is effective but simply because they are in the study. Placebo effects occur when people feel better after some medical treatment because they expect the treatment to work. Hawthorne effects occur when people improve because of the attention they get while participating in a psychological study. Keep these effects in mind as you read in the following article about preliminary studies which suggest that depression is caused by a failure of the left and right hemispheres of the cerebral cortex to communicate properly.

Sandra Blakeslee*
January 19, 1999

Two new theories of depression are rekindling interest in the once fashionable topic of how the left and right sides of the human brain interact.

At a meeting of the Society for Neuroscience last November in Los Angeles, Dr. Jack Pettigrew, a neuroscientist at the University of Queensland in Brisbane, Australia, proposed that people with manic depression have a "sticky switch" somewhere deep in their brains.

In normal people, the switch allows either the left or right hemisphere to be dominant during different mental tasks, with the two sides constantly taking turns. In people with manic depression, one hemisphere becomes locked into a dominant position in periods of depression while the other hemisphere is locked at times of mania. In a truly bizarre finding, Dr. Pettigrew reported that the placement of ice water into one ear seems to unstick the switch.

The second theory is being put forth by Dr. Frederic Schiffer, a psychiatrist at Harvard Medical School. He maintains that one hemisphere can be more immature than the other and that this imbalance leads to different mental disorders. Dr. Schiffer has designed special goggles to help people "talk" to each half of the brain separately, to learn which is less mature, and to bring the two hemispheres into harmony.

Both ideas have been well received by brain lateralization authorities eager to see a revival of their specialty.

"It's nice to see the left and right hemispheres are back," said Dr. Brenda Milner, a cognitive neuroscientist at the Montreal Neurological Institute in Quebec. The notion that the human brain has two halves and that the left side is associated with logical, analytical thinking while the right side is more intuitive, emotional and creative was popularized about 20 years ago, she said, and soon became received wisdom about how the brain works. "This idea fell from fashion not because people didn't like it but because they got interested in other things," she said.

Dr. Marcel Kinsbourne, a cognitive scientist at the New School for Social Research in New York City and early pioneer in brain lateralization studies, believes that left and right brain ideas also fell from fashion because they were oversold. People looked for universal dichotomies—the left brain is a whiz at legal briefs but the right brain is deft at poetry—that carried things too far. But the new theories are "intriguing," Dr. Kinsbourne said, although they have a long way to go before they can be accepted as valid. "We are in half-baked land here," he said.

The new theories are also appealing to many experts because they take on a question that has divided researchers for decades. Do people have one overarching mind that spans the two hemispheres? Or are they born with two separate minds—one on the left and one on the right—which operate so seamlessly that the person simply does not notice that there are two?

The subjective sense of having just one mind is overwhelming and unmistakable, said Dr. Joseph Bogen, a neurosurgeon at the University of Southern California in Los Angeles. But if the thick band of fibers connecting the two hemispheres is severed, he explained, humans seem to end up with two separate minds that show different abilities. In one dramatic disparity, the left hemisphere does all the talking while the mute right hemisphere has better access to emotions. For example, when the right brain is shown a photograph, the talkative left brain will say that it does not see anything and cannot comment. But the left hand, which is connected to the right brain, can raise a thumb up or down in response to the question, "Do you like the picture?"

These kinds of experiments led to a dichotomy of opinion among neuroscientists, Dr. Bogen said. One camp held that in splitting the brain, a single mind is cut into two but that it is abnormal to have two brains. The other camp said every person is born with two brains but because the two sides get along so well, people simply have the illusion of one mind.

After thousands of experiments carried out on normal subjects and split-brain patients, scientists still passionately disagree. But one feature has clearly emerged, said Dr. Terry Sejnowski, a neuroscientist at the Salk Institute in San Diego: Human brains show enormous variation in lateralization.

The claim that certain talents or abilities lie in one hemisphere or the other is usually based on averaging the brains of many people, he said. Because each individual brain is a complex system that evolves in response to a unique environment, many brain functions do not end up in the same place. This is further complicated by the fact that the left and right hemisphere probably communicate through deeper pathways that are not affected in split-brain patients.

The new ideas about lateralization will not resolve the question of one versus two brains, but they do add insights and suggest new ways to treat mental patients, said Dr. Schiffer, whose research was set off by his observation that many of his patients seemed to have a kind of double personality.

"On the one hand, they are very mature and stable, but on the other hand, they can be irrational, overly emotional and compulsive," he said. "Often these two sides appear to struggle against or sabotage each other. The troubled part seems stuck in a traumatic past, whereas the other part seems more mature and in control."

Suspecting he was seeing two minds working at cross purposes, Dr. Schiffer designed a pair of goggles that forced his patients to view the world from either the left or right hemisphere separately.

Many experiments show that it is possible to stimulate one hemisphere and inhibit the other so that a person looks at the world using half a brain at a time, Dr. Schiffer explained. When people gaze to the far right and engage their left brains, they do better on verbal memory tasks, he said, and when they look far to the left, to engage the right brain, they feel more inertia and fatigue.

To test how this affects psychiatric patients, Dr. Schiffer made two types of goggles. One permits vision only in the right visual field, thus activating the left brain. The other allows a person to see objects in the left visual field, which activates the right brain. Each brain hemisphere controls the opposite side of the body.

When patients looked through goggles, they reported very definite feelings, depending on which side of the brain was being engaged, Dr. Schiffer said. Some felt negative symptoms like anxiety and sadness when the right brain was activated. Others felt bad when the left brain was engaged. In general, he said, depressed patients felt worse when the right side was stimulated and people with post-traumatic stress syndrome fared poorly when the left side was more active.

Dr. Schiffer speculates that in certain mental disorders, one hemisphere is less mature than the other. The immature side is the repository of past traumas and can come to dominate the healthy side. Thus each hemisphere has mental properties with some autonomy from the other side. Each can hold separate opinions, have a different sense of human and carry a different perspective on the world.

Many people feel no mood difference when wearing the goggles, Dr. Schiffer said. This may be because both their hemispheres have similar outlooks, being equally calm or equally troubled.

Dr. Schiffer uses the goggles in therapy sessions to help patients recognize their two minds and to help the mature side take control over the immature side. Patients wearing goggles can actually converse with the opposite hemisphere, he said, and through talk therapy work toward recovery. The goggles do not support the idea that the right brain is poetic and the left is logical, Dr. Schiffer said. People are very different. Each hemisphere is individualistic; either one can be messed up or both sides can be in balance.

Dr. Pettigrew, who invented the sticky-switch idea of depression, also falls into the two-minds camp. He theorizes that patients cycle between bouts of mania and depression for days, weeks or months at a time.

"Because the hemispheres have different cognitive styles, I thought it doesn't make sense to have them both working at the same time," Dr.

Pettigrew said in an interview at the neuroscience meeting. "So I thought there should be a switch. This would allow each side to take turns dominating."

Dr. Pettigrew said there was plenty of evidence that different parts of each hemisphere cycle back and forth, left and right, during everyday tasks. Parts of the visual cortex switch dominance every few seconds, he said, whereas parts of the frontal lobes cycle every couple hours.

To measure how fast the two sides switch dominance in a visual task, Dr. Pettigrew used a standard apparatus that measures so-called binocular rivalry. When a target of horizontal lines is shown to the right eye and vertical lines are shown to the left eye, and the targets are flashed, the brain does not fuse the lines into a hatched pattern. One side of the brain sees vertical, the other side sees horizontal and the two take turns seeing a pure target. Most people switch sides every two to three seconds, Dr. Pettigrew said. But patients with manic depression require 20 to 30 seconds to switch between the two targets.

"I think they have a sticky switch between the hemispheres," he said. If the switch is stuck, it may be possible to unstick it, Dr. Pettigrew said, by turning to a strange observation made several years ago by Italian scientists.

"If you tilt a person's head 30 degrees to the side and put ice water into one ear, the opposite brain hemisphere will become activated," he said. Thus cold water in the left ear, activating the right hemisphere, might temporarily reduce the symptoms of mania. Depression might be temporarily reduced by placing cold water in the right ear.

Ice water in the ear is a traditional neurological test that has been performed, among other things, on astronauts in space to help understand space sickness. How ice water stimulates one hemisphere is not precisely known, but it seems to activate orientation pathways in one ear (which tell people where they are in space), and these pathways are connected to mid- and higher-brain regions in the opposite side of the head, Dr. Pettigrew said. Trying the ice water in his own left ear, Dr. Pettigrew, who suffers from manic depression, said, "I sat on my couch at home for 40 hours, ruminating about my life." His left brain was stuck in the depression phase. It was, he said, an unpleasant experience.

Questions

1. What are the implications for split-brain patients of the idea that depression is caused by improper communication between the left and right hemisphere? Is this consistent with what we know about split-brain patients?
2. What assumptions about the function of the two hemispheres of the cortex does Pettigrew's theory of manic depression make? Is this consistent with our knowledge of brain functions?

3. Consider Bogen's example of the split-brain patient who cannot describe images seen in the left visual field verbally (and processed in the right hemisphere) but can indicate with a thumb up or down whether the picture is liked. Does this evidence support the idea that the right brain has better access to emotions?
4. Does Schiffer's description of a person with a double personality convince you that our two hemispheres alternate control over our actions? What additional evidence, if any, would you like to have? Does the description of double personality remind you of anyone you know?
5. Propose a study to test Pettigrew's theory that cold water in the ear can help people who suffer from mania and depression. What control group(s) would you need to include to rule out placebo and Hawthorne effects?

Reading 24

Studies of Schizophrenia Vindicate Psychotherapy

Introduction

Schizophrenia is the prototype of a psychological disorder. Although the term is often misused to refer to multiple personality (or, more formally, dissociative identity disorder), it correctly refers to a class of disorders characterized by a disconnection from reality. Common symptoms of schizophrenia include hallucinations (especially auditory hallucinations), delusions (e.g., of grandeur or of paranoia), and inappropriate affect (either inappropriately intense or inappropriately flat). These symptoms can be classified into two types: positive and negative. "Positive" symptoms are not those that are good to have; "positive" here refers to the presence of things that most people do not have. Hallucinations and delusions are good examples of positive symptoms. "Negative" symptoms refers to things that are missing in schizophrenia that most people do have. Lack of emotion or social skills are examples of negative symptoms.

Antipsychotic drugs such as Thorazine have been the preferred treatment for schizophrenia for decades. Thorazine—which works by blocking dopamine receptors—is an effective treatment for most positive symptoms of schizophrenia, but is ineffective in reducing negative symptoms. In other words, with current methods we can take away the hallucinations and delusions brought on by the disorder, but we cannot yet give back the emotions and social skills that were taken away. The following reading describes a study testing a new type of treatment for schizophrenia. The results are striking in showing a reduction in negative symptoms. Equally striking is that this new treatment is a type of psychotherapy, perhaps the first psychotherapy to be demonstrably effective in treating schizophrenia.

Denise Grady*
January 20, 1998

When a man with schizophrenia requested psychotherapy recently in addition to his antipsychotic medication, he was told that his health maintenance organization would allow only six sessions. "The insurer said there was no evidence that psychotherapy helps people with schizophrenia," said Gerard Hogarty, a researcher and professor of psychiatry at the University of Pittsburgh School of Medicine.

The story is all too familiar to therapists. The notion behind it is that people with schizophrenia are either too sick to be reached by psychotherapy or, thanks to medication, too well to need it.

But Professor Hogarty and his research team have shown that schizophrenic patients taking medication can be helped further by a certain type of psychotherapy. In two studies published in November in *The American Journal of Psychiatry,* the group showed that a three-year course of the treatment, which they developed and named personal therapy, was extremely helpful to many patients in preventing relapses and improving social adjustment.

Dr. Wayne Fenton, medical director of Chestnut Lodge Hospital in Rockville, Md., who was an author of an editorial accompanying the results of the studies, said they provided the first scientific proof that psychotherapy can help people with schizophrenia. "Because of this, people can no longer argue that psychotherapy for schizophrenia is not effective," Dr. Fenton said. "One might say there is no excuse anymore not to provide needed care."

Although antipsychotic drugs are unmatched in their power to halt the hallucinations and delusions that characterize schizophrenia, they do not erase all signs of illness.

"People are better, but not well," Professor Hogarty said. Despite medication, many patients still have difficulties with memory, attention, problem solving and relating to other people. Relapses are common, often because patients quit taking their medication, but sometimes even when they stick with it. Only 10 percent to 30 percent of the two million Americans with schizophrenia are employed. "There's no drug out there to teach you how to get along with anybody, or how to get a job and keep one," Professor Hogarty said.

Dr. George T. Niederehe, head of the adult and geriatric psychosocial treatment research program at the National Institute of Mental Health, said, "Many of the people we talk about as the homeless are persons with these kinds of mental health problems."

Dr. Niederehe and other experts praised the study. "It's a major advance," said Dr. William T. Carpenter Jr., director of the Maryland Psychiatric Research Center in Baltimore. Dr. Carpenter, who was not associated with the study, said that personal therapy appeared to be the most beneficial treatment developed since the first antipsychotic drugs were introduced in the 1950's.

The treatment of schizophrenia has had a contentious history. When it became clear during the 1960's that antipsychotic drugs worked far better than psychotherapy for most patients, doctors began to question whether psychotherapy was of any use for people with schizophrenia. There are about 400 different types of psychotherapy, Professor Hogarty said, and studies in the last 30 years have been contradictory, with some finding psychotherapy helpful in treating schizophrenia and others calling it useless or even harmful.

By the mid-1980's, psychotherapy had such a bad reputation among experts in schizophrenia that a proposal to study anything by that name would have been "an invitation to unemployment," Professor Hogarty said. The climate inspired him and his colleagues to call the techniques they developed something else: personal therapy.

Their treatment differs radically from the Freudian psychoanalysis that many people think of as psychotherapy. "We're not looking into suppressed thoughts about Mama," Professor Hogarty said. "It's more in the here and now."

Personal therapy is based on the idea that people with schizophrenia are born with brain abnormalities that make them especially vulnerable to emotional stress. Overwhelming stress, often from dealings with other people, can lead to anxiety and depression, which may in turn spiral down into psychosis.

In personal therapy, the therapist tries initially to help patients recognize stress and manage it in order to avoid relapses of schizophrenia. The treatment program is tailored to each patient's needs, and patients progress at their own pace. Eventually, they may reach a stage where they are ready for counseling to help them get along better with other people and to minimize stressful encounters.

Professor Hogarty's study included 151 patients, 97 living with their families and 54 living independently. Most were in their 20's or 30's, and all took antipsychotic medication. Each was assigned to a group that received personal therapy two to four times a month for three years, or, for comparison, family therapy, personal and family therapy, or supportive therapy in which patients were given the opportunity to talk with a therapist and seek help during crises.

In the patients who lived with relatives, only a quarter who received personal therapy alone had relapses, as opposed to half of those who had the other kinds of therapy. Only two quit personal therapy, but 13 dropped out of the other programs.

But in patients living on their own, more receiving personal therapy had relapses than those getting supportive treatment: about half relapsed, as opposed to slightly more than a third of the others. Four left personal therapy, and five left supportive therapy. The researchers said they suspected that personal therapy failed in that group because many of the patients were struggling to find housing, food and clothing, and the treatment may have been too demanding for them.

But in another area, social adjustment, both groups of patients benefited from personal therapy. Personal relationships and work performance improved. Most important, they continued to get better over time, while benefits from the other types of therapy tended to reach a plateau after a year. Had the study gone on, Professor Hogarty said, the patients in personal therapy might have continued to improve even further.

He and his team have devised another treatment that they are now testing, called cognitive enhancement therapy. It involves computer programs aimed at helping patients improve problem-solving skills, and group sessions designed to heighten the ability to act wisely in social situations. Patients like it, and Professor Hogarty thinks the treatment may ultimately prove even more helpful than personal therapy.

Despite the value of personal therapy, other researchers and Professor Hogarty himself said they doubted it would come into widespread use. It is expensive and time-consuming, and would require extensive retraining of therapists.

Nonetheless, Professor Hogarty said, in the long run personal therapy might prove cost effective, because by preventing relapses it can keep patients out of the hospital, which is the most expensive form of care. The treatment may also get them back in the work force. "You get what you pay for," he said. "If you want to pay something more, the lives of these patients can improve substantially."

Questions

1. Are antipsychotic drugs more effective in eliminating the positive or negative symptoms of schizophrenia?
2. Hogarty says that insurers claim schizophrenics are either too sick to be reached by psychotherapy or because of antipsychotic drugs too well to need it. How should this statement be modified according to his new data?
3. Averaging the relapse rates of patients who lived alone and those that lived with relatives, how did personal therapy compare with supportive therapy?
4. Briefly outline Hogarty's study of personal therapy. Did this study control for placebo and Hawthorne effects?
5. Why does Hogarty think that personal therapy will not be widely used? If you managed an insurance company, based on these results would you recommend that your company pay for personal therapy?

Reading 25

"Memory" Therapy Leads to a Lawsuit and Big Settlement

Introduction

Our final reading addresses one of the most contentious issues in all of psychology today: recovered memories. Recovered memories (which are often called "repressed memories" by those who believe in their accuracy and "false memories" by those who do not) gained national attention when Eileen Franklin testified in 1989 to having witnessed her father George Franklin murder her close friend Susan Nason in 1969. Eileen said that she repressed the memory of the crime for 20 years and it had only recently come back to her. She initially said that the memory came back to her during a hypnosis session with her therapists but later said that it came back while at home looking at her daughter. Despite the lack of any other evidence, George Franklin was convicted of the crime.

At the time of the case, many cognitive psychologists were troubled because there was no evidence that memory could work in the way that Eileen described. Yet many clinical psychologists, particularly those following a neo-Freudian, psychodynamic orientation, did believe that memories could be repressed. Since that time psychologists have argued—often heatedly—over what to make of recovered memories. Cognitive psychologists have gained some ground by showing that recovered memories can be wholly inaccurate. But knowing that recovered memories can be inaccurate does not necessarily mean they are never accurate. Still, courts today are much less likely to accept recovered memories as evidence, and George Franklin was released from prison on appeal. As reported in Pam Belluck's article, the legal tide against accepting recovered memories as genuine is turning even further: Now some clinicians who have diagnosed patients in the past as having repressed memories are being sued by those same patients. And in just about every case so far, the courts are finding against clinicians.

Pam Belluck*
November 6, 1997

While undergoing psychiatric therapy at a Chicago hospital from 1986 to 1992, Patricia Burgus says, she was convinced by doctors that she had memories of being part of a satanic cult, being sexually abused by numerous men and abusing her own two sons.

She says that hypnosis and other treatments caused her to believe she remembered cannibalizing people, so much so that her husband brought in a hamburger from a family picnic and therapists agreed to test the meat to see if it was human.

Today lawyers for Mrs. Burgus said that insurance companies for two doctors and the hospital, Rush-Presbyterian-St. Luke's, had agreed to pay $10.6 million, the biggest settlement in a lawsuit alleging that therapists had instilled false memories and part of a growing legal backlash against therapies that try to elicit suppressed recollections.

Treatment that focuses on recovered memories gained popularity in the 1980's and over the last decade or so, recollections of abuse and other traumatic experiences have been the basis for lawsuits and criminal cases. Six years ago, a jury in Redwood City, Calif., convicted a man of raping and murdering his daughter's playmate in 1969, based largely on the daughter's latent recollections.

But recently the tide has been turning away from accepting the validity of these recovered memories.

Three years ago, the American Psychiatric Association cautioned that such memories were often not true and expressed skepticism about using hypnosis and other techniques to help elicit them. Judges have recently suppressed testimony based on recovered memories. And a growing number of patients have won lawsuits against such therapists.

At least 20 such lawsuits have been filed in the last two years, with the plaintiffs being successful in virtually all the ones that have been completed.

In 1996, a church in Missouri agreed to pay $1 million to a woman who said that under the guidance of a church counselor, she came to believe that her father had raped her, got her pregnant and performed a coat-hanger

*Reprinted with permission from *The New York Times.*

abortion—when in fact, she was still a virgin and her father had had a vasectomy. And in August, a jury awarded $5.8 million to a woman in Houston who said her psychotherapist had implanted memories of murder, satanism and cannibalism.

Last week, in a related Houston case, a Federal grand jury brought what are believed to be the first criminal charges in such a case. The indictment charges that a hospital administrator and four therapists collected millions of dollars in fraudulent insurance payments by exaggerating patients' diagnoses and inducing false memories of being part of a satanic cult.

"As in most crazes, it has produced its damage and most people are coming to see the kinds of problems it represents," said Dr. Paul R. McHugh, chairman of the department of psychiatry at the Johns Hopkins School of Medicine and a consultant for Mrs. Burgus.

"Could there have been someone who is abused and not remember it? I'm not saying that that's not possible. I'm saying first that these memories can never be validated without corroborating evidence. And secondly it's a slippery slope opening the door for these conspiracy theories about satanic cults and alien abductions."

A spokesman for Rush-Presbyterian, John Pontarelli, said officials there would not comment on the settlement, in which none of the parties admitted wrongdoing. The psychiatrist who treated Mrs. Burgus's sons from 1986 to 1989, Dr. Elva Poznanski, the hospital's section chief of child and adolescent psychiatry, issued a statement saying, "On the basis of the knowledge available at that time, I would not change the treatment of these boys."

Mrs. Burgus's sons were hospitalized starting at the ages of 4 and 5, and subjected, she says, to disturbing therapy sessions, including one that involved seeing if they knew how to use handcuffs and a gun in an effort to verify what doctors suspected might be abusive incidents.

The other psychiatrist, Dr. Bennett G. Braun, director of the hospital's section of psychiatric trauma, today called the settlement a "travesty" and said that it was done over his objections.

"A patient comes into the hospital doing so bad that she belongs in the hospital and after several serious events in the hospital which I can't disclose because of patient confidentiality, she was discharged and is doing much better," he said. "Where's the damage?"

Dr. Braun said Mrs. Burgus raised the stories herself. "She just spit it out," he said. "All of the cult stuff that she was talking about I learned from her. The idea to bring the meat in was hers. I merely said if he does bring it in, I will try to get it analyzed for human protein. Yes the kids did see handcuffs. They did see a gun. But it was for therapeutic reasons."

He said Mrs. Burgus had exaggerated the use of hypnotism in treating her. "I'm not disagreeing with some of the things she says. It's just the slant."

Dr. Braun, 57, was the founding president of the International Society for the Study of Dissociation, which looks at theories of multiple personality and the idea that parts of the mind can dissociate certain experiences from other parts of the mind.

Dr. Elizabeth S. Bowman, an associate professor of psychiatry at the University of Indiana in Indianapolis and a past-president of the society, said that such therapists "firmly believe that people forget trauma, there's no question that memories return, and that some of the memories that return are accurate."

But Dr. Bowman said "the field has become more cautious because of lawsuits and we also with time are gaining more awareness that these memories sometimes are accurate and sometimes are not. We do try to educate patients about that."

Mrs. Burgus, 41, said in an interview that she was referred to the hospitals by therapists in her hometown of Des Moines who had been treating her for what she describes as a severe post-partum depression. She said she received a diagnosis of multiple personality disorder and was treated with various medications, hypnosis and was occasionally kept in leather restraints during six years of treatment, two and a half years as an inpatient. She said her children were hospitalized because doctors believed her disorder might be genetic.

She said she decided to file suit when, after getting out of the hospital, "I started to check out certain things that we had now based our lives on, these horror stories. I couldn't find any proof of anything."

Across the country in the last two years, other cases have been filed, many of them alleging similarly bizarre or violent memories. In 1995, a jury in Minnesota awarded $2.6 million to a woman who claimed her St. Paul psychiatrist told her that if she recovered her buried memories she would discover that she had been sexually abused by relatives.

"The next thing I think there will be is legislation to force informed consent by psychiatric patients for this treatment," said Dr. R. Christopher Barden, a psychologist and a lawyer, who worked on Mrs. Burgus's case. "I think insurance companies will stop reimbursing people for mental health treatments not proven safe and effective. This is the death knell for recovered memory therapy."

Questions

1. What is a repressed memory? How does repressing differ from forgetting?
2. If the children had no explicit memory of handling guns and handcuffs, why did the therapist show them these items to see whether

they could handle them properly? Does this seem to you a valid technique?

3. Was it appropriate for Braun to agree to Burgus's request to have a hamburger analyzed for human protein? How else might he have coped with her fear that she was eating other humans?
4. Braun was using techniques that are accepted by many practicing psychologists, and Burgus's depression improved during the six-year therapy. What, then, is the basis of her lawsuit? How would you have decided in this case?
5. Based on your understanding of the controversy surrounding recovered memories, would you ever allow them to be admitted as evidence in a legal case? Would you always allow them to be admitted? Outline a research program that could increase our understanding of these issues.